Parenting a Child with Arthritis

Also by Earl J. Brewer, Jr., M.D.:
Juvenile Rheumatoid Arthritis
(with Edward H. Giannini, Dr.P.H., and Donald Person, M.D.)

Parenting a Child with Arthritis

A Practical, Empathetic Guide to Help You and Your Child Live with Arthritis

Earl J. Brewer, Jr., M.D.
and
Kathy Cochran Angel

LOWELL HOUSE
Los Angeles

CONTEMPORARY BOOKS
Chicago

KATHY

This book is dedicated to my mother, who allowed me to be myself.
To John, Virginia, and Elizabeth, who taught me so much.
And to Gary, for doing his best to keep me organized.

EARL

To Ria, the best of the best. With such apparent ease,
she makes everything possible.

Library of Congress Cataloging-in-Publication Data

Brewer, Earl J., 1928-
  Parenting a child with arthritis: a practical, empathetic guide to help you and
  your child live with arthritis/Earl J. Brewer, Jr., and Kathy Cochran Angel.
      p.   cm.
  Includes bibliographical references and index.
  ISBN 0-929923-55-3
  1. Rheumatoid arthritis in children—Popular works. I. Angel, Kathy
  Cochran. II. Title.
  RJ482.A77B74 1992
  362.1'98927227—dc20   91-36064
                                                             CIP

Lowell House
2029 Century Park East, Suite 3290
Los Angeles, CA 90067

Publisher: Jack Artenstein
General Manager, Lowell House Adult: Bud Sperry
Design: Nancy Freeborn

Manufactured in the United States of America
10 9 8 7 6 5 4 3 2 1

Contents

Finding the Right College or Trade School
Planning the Future

Foreword

After leaving the post of Surgeon General which I held for eight years, I still take the greatest satisfaction in a program I was privileged to direct that redesigned the ways in which children with special health needs—this includes juvenile rheumatoid arthritis (JRA)—could take advantage of the programs in the tangled web of health care and social service agencies that exist for their benefit. Earl Brewer worked with me in this effort for several years. The information given to you in this book is directly related to our joint concern to help you get the best care for your child.

Earl comes to this effort with over 30 years of competent and compassionate care for children with JRA and their families. Kathy Angel is a caring and capable mother who has been through the experience of parenting a child with JRA from childhood through adolescence into adulthood. This is the first book to my knowledge that takes the child with JRA from the initial shock of diagnosis to the transition to adulthood. It is complete, from appropriate exercises to proper nutrition, from team care to medications, and from family support to school problems. Both authors tell it like it is and are upbeat while doing so. *Parenting a Child with Arthritis* gives enough information for you to make informed choices about doctors and teaches you how to be a partner in the care of your child. Until we learn to prevent JRA, this book will be of great benefit to anyone who must deal with its effects on children and their families.

C. Everett Koop, M.D.
Bethesda, Maryland

For the thing I greatly feared is come upon me.
JOB

From the Authors

KATHY

There are moments in our lives that will always remain indelible in our memories. Ask people where they were when the astronauts landed on the moon and they will give you a vivid recollection. Where were they when John Kennedy was shot? When their first child was born?

For me, the moment when an orthopedic surgeon called to tell me my youngest child, then 11 years old, in all probability had rheumatoid arthritis, is one of those moments. I was sitting on the edge of my bed, looking out the window at the magnificent oak trees surrounding my home in Houston. Could he possibly be talking about my Elizabeth? My bubbly, mischievous, vivacious child? She was swimming, she was playing tennis, she was so full of enthusiasm. Surely there was some mistake.

Overcoming our tremendous anxiety, our search for the best medical care we could find led us to Dr. Earl J. Brewer, Jr., in the Texas Medical Center. Through his efforts, his health team's expertise, our family's commitment, and Elizabeth's determination, the future looks bright indeed for my child. Today she is finishing her university degree and deciding her future directions. Without the collaboration I described above this story would have had a much different ending.

My desire to write this book with Earl stems from a sincere belief that through education, through cooperation between the patient, the family members, and the health professionals, the prognosis for children with rheumatic diseases improves markedly. With an acute illness the role of the physician is to prescribe medication, to recommend surgical intervention, to direct. When the illness is chronic the relationship between patient, physician, and family is dramatically altered. I would illustrate the relationship by describing the family as the hub of a wheel. The spokes radiating out are all the people partic-ipating in the effort to heal the child: the physician, the nurse, the physical therapist, the occupational therapist, the nutritionist, and so on. The spokes may change from time to time as needs dictate, but the core, the family, remains constant.

We hope that this book will be helpful to you. By sharing our experiences, by learning from each other, by discovering that we are not alone, that we can indeed make a difference in the life of a child, we can grow enormously. We all have the potential to improve the lives of our children. All it takes is a dogged determination, a dedica-tion born of love, and a sense of humor!

Kathy Angel
Los Angeles, California
July 9, 1991

EARL

When Kathy Angel called to ask if I would write a book with her to share our experiences with parents, siblings, and children with arthri-tis, it took about one minute for me to accept. There is no one more appropriate than Kathy to share the proper information and attitudes necessary to help families to understand, cope, and access services better. In life it is often difficult to know what is the right thing to do. We usually know, however, what is the wrong thing to do. This book is for you as a parent, not for medical professionals. Our goal is to be your friend, guiding you about the right things to do and warning you about the wrong things to do.

When Elizabeth developed arthritis, Kathy immediately mobi-lized her forces and said, "What do we need to do?" All of us feel the anger, hurt, and frustration when serious problems happen to our children. In one way or another, we deny that it has happened and then feel sick about the whole thing. Hopefully at some point all of us pull ourselves up by the boot straps and say, "Let's get on with it."

As well as being your helper and friend who has been down the trail before you, this book is about getting on with it, and more important, about what you want to happen to your child and family years later when your child grows up. Most children with arthritis develop normally and have little difficulty as adults; unfortunately, early in the disease, we never really know which children need the most help. So you need to do your best from the beginning.

Earl J. Brewer, Jr., M.D.
Houston, Texas
July 9, 1991

Authors' Note

Most children with JRA are girls, but many are boys. To get around writing "she/he" every time we mention a child with JRA, we'll use "she." Concerning adults and professionals, we've used "he" or "she" with no intent to favor either. We like boys and girls equally well.

In writing this book together we found that our writing styles are sufficiently different and that you will immediately know who is talking at any given time. When there might be any doubt, we'll identify the speaker.

Acknowledgments

Our thanks and appreciation to the following:

Janice Gallagher, editor and friend, who taught us a great deal during the writing of this book and even more for the future.

Lowell House, for giving us the opportunity to reach out to parents of children with JRA.

Pat Harrington, Vice President of the Arthritis Foundation, for helping us assemble many resources for you and your child; also for reading the final manuscript.

Edward Giannini, Dr.P.H., and Dan Lovell, M.D., M.P.H., for reading the final manuscript and for listening and offering advice on what parents need to learn.

James Cassidy, M.D., Patience White, M.D., Balu Athreya, M.D., and Linda Dutton, for reading the final manuscript and listening so patiently and offering advice.

Gaye Koenning, M.S., R.D., for helpful advice about the team and a helpful list of nutritional pamphlets.

Edith Shear, M.S.W., for sharing the Resource Directory she prepared for the American Juvenile Arthritis Organization (AJAO) of the Arthritis Foundation.

1

Wrestling with the Angel: Kathy's Story

On a beautiful spring day in 1980, I received a call from Elizabeth's school. She had fallen on the playground, her ankle was swollen, and I should pick her up. By evening her ankle was the size of a grapefruit. The following day, X-rays at the hospital revealed no fracture. The doctor wrapped the ankle, gave her a pain medication, and recommended that she stay off it and come back in a few days. Six weeks later the ankle was still the same size, and X-rays still revealed no fracture. She was in a lace-up supporting boot and limping badly.

But more ominous signs had begun to appear. Swelling began in several joints of her hands. The orthopedic surgeon, a family friend, called me on that spring day to tell me of his suspicions that Elizabeth might have a juvenile rheumatic disease. I did not even know that children could get arthritis. It's an "old person's disease." My grandmother ended her life in a wheelchair with rheumatoid arthritis. Her daughter, my aunt, was severely crippled with rheumatoid arthritis. I indeed lived in fear of contracting the disease myself, a fear I had not shared with anyone. But my baby, my Elizabeth! Impossible!

But as part of a medical family, I knew that denying the diagnosis would not change the facts. My former husband, a physician, began to survey his colleagues, the medical literature, drug reps, and anyone he could to find the best possible medical care for our daughter. I inquired of my friends in Houston. To our great joy, the person most recommended was five minutes from our house, in the Texas Medical Center. Earl J. Brewer, Jr., M.D., was the person to see.

Surely They're Not Talking About My Daughter!

In an absolute daze I made the initial appointment. Torn between "surely it will go away tomorrow" (Scarlett O'Hara) and "we will find a cure for this" (Katharine Hepburn), I plodded on in pain and disbelief. There was a brief encounter with Dr. Brewer, who had the onerous duty of explaining the disease and the possible ramifications for Elizabeth. I knew that the physician must necessarily give you the worst-case scenario — describe all the possibilities — but he was talking about my child in a way that I found totally unacceptable. I had an overwhelming urge to throw this rather large man out his 10th-floor window. How dare he say these horrible things about my child! My daughter would not be crippled! My daughter would not be in a wheelchair! I was furious, horrified. I would prove him wrong!

We then went for an all-day series of laboratory and X-ray tests. During lunch, Elizabeth paused and said she would make a deal with me. She would take the 16 baby aspirins a day, without arguing, if I would just PLEASE stop crying. I had to smile, and that was a deal I could not pass up. We finished the day with a visit to the ophthalmologist.

Several days and many baby aspirins later, we returned to Dr. Brewer's office for the results of the tests. He examined Elizabeth again, reviewed the tests, and began to explain again the reality of juvenile rheumatic disease: "It will take some time to reach a definitive diagnosis." Translation: the diagnosis of arthritis is a process of elimination. There is no specific test to tell you that you have rheumatoid arthritis. There are indicators. There are symptoms. In Elizabeth's case, she became so ill, so fast, that for six months they weren't sure she did not have leukemia or lupus. Those were six of the most difficult months of my life.

Juvenile rheumatoid arthritis does not only involve the joints. It may affect the eyes, the heart, and just about any organ in the body.

Since it's an autoimmune disease, the body is basically attacking itself. And attack Elizabeth it did. I've never seen a person deteriorate so rapidly.

Aspirin, something we all have in our medicine cabinets, was the first drug that was tried when Elizabeth developed her arthritis. It can work wonders. As innocuous as aspirin seems in our daily lives, however, it can have serious side effects. Initially, it was controlling Elizabeth's pain and inflammation. She was going at least once a week for blood tests to monitor the effects of the aspirin. When lab tests showed that Elizabeth's liver was being damaged by the large doses needed to control her arthritis, we had to stop the aspirin.

Within 24 hours she was bedridden, screaming in pain. I could not believe what was happening. She was in such severe pain that no one could touch her. This was probably the moment in which the stark reality of the situation came full force into my brain. I was terrified! I wanted to take her pain into my body. I couldn't. It took about a week for the aspirin to be completely out of her system. Then began the search for a medication that could control the arthritis symptoms without doing permanent damage to her liver or kidneys, or creating other serious side effects.

Juvenile rheumatic diseases are extremely difficult both to diagnose and to treat. The severity of the disease varies widely from child to child. There are many drugs available to try to control the symptoms. But each individual reacts differently, one drug being very beneficial to one child and useless to another. The diagnosis is a process of elimination, and finding the right medication is also a tedious process of elimination. And to complicate the matter further, a medication that works one day may become totally ineffective overnight. In a period of five years Elizabeth took 13 different drugs, some of them experimental, with a tremendous variety of responses. Some of them did nothing. Some helped but had really serious side effects. The balance is so delicate.

In those early months it was necessary to go each week to the doctor and the laboratory. I began to dread those days. I can only imagine what they inspired in Elizabeth. Her veins were so fragile and the weekly blood tests began to take their toll on her tiny arms. She became knowledgeable very fast about the routines of laboratory testing.

All in the Family

Within one month after the initial appointment with Earl, Elizabeth was pretty much confined to bed. She had 46 joints inflamed and was in extreme pain. I can only try to describe the impact that this sudden, dramatic change has on each member of a family.

A wonderful man, James May, a psychologist from Washington state who has had arthritis since his early teen years, describes the family as a mobile, gently swaying in the breeze. Each member of the family contributes to the overall balance. When everything is in harmony, the mobile is fine. When there is disharmony, when one part collapses, things begin to go awry.

Frequently a child who develops arthritis will suffer a tremendous loss of self-esteem. Perhaps she has been a good athlete and now can no longer compete. Her self-image may change dramatically. Depression is a very common occurrence in a child with a chronic illness.

And the impact on the parents is profound, too. All parents expect to have a "perfect" child. It seems to me that fathers have a particularly difficult time with this initially. We frequently have a very narcissistic belief that our children are mere extensions of ourselves. I can assure you that their accomplishments will be unique to them, and their problems will also be unique. It's difficult to separate ourselves, and often the father is not included in the daily care of the child. He begins to feel that his only role is that of "breadwinner." Who among us would like to be valued only for the amount of money we earn? Since mothers are usually the primary caretaker, their life interests are often put on hold, and sometimes never recovered. In my case, Elizabeth was recovering long before I began to recover. As a matter of fact, she helped me to regain my life.

Siblings, also part of the mobile, often feel neglected because of the attention given to the sick child. There is a tremendous frustration level because we all want to help—but how? Yet we also have our own emotional needs. As a family you need to look honestly at all of these feelings to restructure the balance of your relationships and regain your family harmony.

As far as cousins, aunts, uncles, my mother, and friends, they really seemed to have a difficult, if not impossible time seeing Elizabeth in such pain. It really took a while before they accepted the facts.

However, it didn't take long for the immediate family to accept the situation. When Elizabeth was awakening in pain each morning, going through the entire day in pain, and awakening each night in pain, we were all affected. You simply cannot live with that kind of chronic suffering and not be changed in many ways. It becomes the focus of your day. How do you eliminate it? All other cares become very secondary.

The Team

When Earl realized that Elizabeth could not tolerate the aspirin and that the disease was rapidly becoming worse, he sat me down one day and explained what we should expect. "Elizabeth does not have a little arthritis. She has a lot of arthritis. By the time we have this under control you will all feel as if you had been through the Third World War." What a prophet! This is the point in time when the availability of a very specialized health care team becomes extremely important. You have accepted the reality of the disease process. What you need now is the ammunition to proceed with the battle.

Most physicians are extremely busy. The better they are the busier they are. They cannot spend hours with families educating them on the multiple details of these diseases. The concept of team care becomes very important in the treatment of a chronic illness. (Please see Appendix A: List of Pediatric Rheumatologists and Appendix B: Directory of Pediatric Rheumatology Centers for lists of specialized doctors and clinics located all across the country.)

Elizabeth saw a number of doctors and other health care professionals in the course of her illness. Her eyes had to be checked regularly for inflammation. She developed several heart murmurs that had to be checked periodically by a cardiologist. We also got to know the orthopedic surgeon quite well. Physical therapy was one of the most important factors (in my opinion) in her treatment. The occupational therapist gave her the splints to try to minimize the displacement of her joints, and the nurse was there to answer our daily questions. Having multiple resources was a tremendous help to me.

While the doctors and health professionals search for the most effective means to treat your child, you must maintain your child in many other areas. One of the most important is her mental state. You become a cheerleader. I lived in mortal fear of the day that Elizabeth would wake up and say, "I can't do this. I just want to stay in bed and forget all this nonsense." Thank God she never did. I attribute this in great part to the love and support of everyone around her. Beginning with the family, and including her friends and the medical team that guided us, she always knew she was not alone in her effort.

Your child will need your help to remember to take the medication. How much help she needs is largely a factor of her age. With younger children the problems may be: first, convincing them of the necessity of taking it; second, overcoming the difficulty of swallowing some of the pills; third, creating a schedule to remember the proper time and incorporating it into your life-style.

With older children you need to encourage them to assume responsibility for taking their medications regularly and on time. They should probably keep a written schedule of time and type of medication taken. It really is important for them to begin controlling their own environment. They are the ones who will suffer by not following directions. If they forget the medication, THEY will be the ones who are unable to get out of bed the next morning. I assure you they will get the message.

The other contribution families make is to help maintain the strength of muscles through physical therapy. With this kind of pain the first thought is to put your child to bed. Wrong! It is imperative to keep the affected joints moving and as strong as possible. When Earl first saw Elizabeth, her right arm was frozen at 45 degrees of motion. Obviously, she had had this problem for some time. Since I consider myself a conscientious parent, I felt tremendous guilt. I should have recognized the problem. I did not. OK, so what do we do now? Earl explained that there were no definitive studies on the effectiveness of physical therapy in children. He said, "I can't assure you that it will help. But I can assure you that if you don't do it she will probably be in a wheelchair soon."

What a way to get your attention! Seeing my child unable to straighten her arm was all the incentive I needed. I was definitely motivated. Within one month her mobility in the right arm had improved markedly because of the physical therapy. It was very dramatic and I feel it offered us the encouragement we needed to continue actively with the very painful exercises.

Most Unexpected Gifts

As I reflect on the early days of Elizabeth's disease, and as I examine the processes that went on in my family, I must confess that I am frequently reduced to tears. It was an impossible time for all of us, but as this introspective process goes on I find that I am also able to recall the positive things that evolved as a result of what was happening around and to us. Some days Elizabeth could "almost" walk. We discovered that to conserve my back, she could stand in front of me, with her back to me, stand on my feet, my arms around her, and we had the makings of a great vaudeville act. As we strolled to our destination we sang things like "Me and My Shadow" or perhaps "We Ain't Got a Barrel of Money." I always smile when I hear one of "our" songs.

We became very close. We spent so much time together we began to know what the other was thinking. We finished each other's sentences. Not many parents have the opportunity to develop that kind of a relationship with their children.

Mobility was, of course, a problem. We were determined not to resort to a wheelchair unless it was absolutely necessary. It is so easy to become dependent on them. We preferred to let life slow down, to accommodate Elizabeth's pace on any given day.

Some days were much better than others. Initially, she would apologize for "slowing us down." I began to realize that there were certain advantages to taking life more slowly. I saw things that I had not noticed in my usual haste. So when Elizabeth apologized for the inconvenience she was causing, I explained to her that I was actually enjoying seeing the world in a different perspective. She hugged me!

Several years later, when she was much better, we went to Europe. I became extremely ill and we had to return home early. When we got to the airport in Paris, I could hardly walk. I told the rest of the family to hurry ahead to check in with the airline. Elizabeth insisted on staying by my side. She reminded me that when she could not walk I had always stayed by her side. Yes, I am crying.

If you meet Elizabeth today you would probably not realize that she has, and has had, serious arthritis for many years. The road to this point has been complicated and circuitous. It has not been easy, and it may not be over yet. But I have faith in her ability to take the challenges of each day and accomplish wonderful things. She may "have arthritis," but she is not "arthritic." She is a vibrant, active, involved person and I know she will live life to the fullest.

Today Elizabeth has graduated from the university with a degree in psychology. She is making future plans with all the optimism of youth. Her future is indeed bright. She still has the arthritis but it is controlled with medication. She occasionally has problems with it, usually related to stress. She understands and is working to control the stress of daily life. If we had lived in a rural area, without access to a large, sophisticated medical center and caring health professionals, our lives would have been much more complicated by this disease, and this story might have had a much different ending. I know for certain that the road would have been much more difficult.

To my joy one of the goals of the pediatric rheumatologists has been to somehow establish outreach clinics to help families in rural areas and smaller towns, to help the local pediatricians in the treatment of these diseases. One goal in writing this book is to encourage families to get help by any means. I would hope that if we had not been able to control the damage to her body, Elizabeth would still be the same charming, optimistic young lady that she is today. Being her mother, I feel sure that is the case. The children I have met around the country who have had to deal with arthritis are, in general, an articulate, strong-willed, courageous group, irrespective of their degrees of physical impairment. They are mature beyond their years. They tend to be more compassionate than the average child. God works in strange ways.

In this book we will try to give you a broad picture of many of the problems you might encounter in dealing with juvenile arthritis. Dr. Brewer is a respected authority in the field and can explain exactly what arthritis is and its impact on your child. We will explain the medications available to help.

We hope to give you an idea of methods to improve the quality of life not only for your child but for your family. There are incredible resources to help you through the maze of the educational system. There are wonderful support groups to do just that—support you. We will tell you about them. I hope the following chapters will give you guidance and hope in your efforts to help your child into a happy, productive future. There is no other pain quite like seeing your child in pain and being unable to alleviate it in some way. To live with it over long periods of time will change you forever. Once you have "wrestled with the angel" you will hopefully emerge a stronger, more focused human being. Having the experiences I did with Elizabeth gave me a whole different perspective on life. We all have a spiritual side to our nature. It is sometimes lost in the everyday rush. The hours you devote to helping your child conquer this disease will strengthen you in ways no one can anticipate.

2

What Is Juvenile Rheumatoid Arthritis?

You're sitting in my exam room, all 8 by 10 of it, looking out of the window from the 10th floor at a canyon of cement and bricks, worrying that your family's world is coming to an end. You cross and uncross your legs, wondering how far away is the damn rest room and, if you go, whether you'll miss his eminence, Dr. Earl. You decide to wait it out and cross your knees one more time. On the wall you see a poster board with a sign, JRA KIDS. In mindless boredom you look at school and home snapshots of a hundred happy, smiling children. Lo and behold, most of the pictures are of the same children taken years apart. There are even pictures of these kids grown up with children of their own.

You suddenly get it: "Hey, this is the best news I've had all day. I'm in the right place." And that's how I want you to feel after reading this chapter: "Hey, this is the best news I've had all day. I'm in the right place."

There's nothing worse than when someone tells you how a book ends, but to save wear and tear on your psyche, you need to know that kids with JRA grow up, go to college, get jobs, marry, and have children, and few have big problems with arthritis. However, much of what happens in between depends on you and your child.

So what is JRA? Let's talk about it.

Currently we estimate that about one in 1,000 children in the United States has JRA. That multiplies to about 60,000. It's certainly as common as diabetes. In my experience the figures are probably about the same in other parts of the world.

Children with JRA have arthritis of the joints for six weeks or longer. Having arthritis means a joint is swollen or painful and limited in motion. Having arthritis means that when you look at a joint, it's puffy or red; or when touched, the joint is warm, and if you move it your child jumps a little with pain. Any joint in the body can have arthritis. JRA also can cause problems in other parts of the body. We'll talk about that as we go along.

What Causes JRA?

We don't know. Many theories—no answers. There is certainly some, if not more, genetic predisposition in some kids with JRA; the immune system and defense system of the body somehow are not working properly; and infection as a triggering mechanism can't be dismissed.

Can you remember the beginning of JRA in your family? Of course you can. In other families there have been some events that seem to happen too often to say, "Who the blup cares?" Here are a few.

We know there are many associated or predisposing factors. Increasing knowledge of genes and gene markers points to the probability that inherited genes predispose to some types of JRA. In 30 years of practice, I saw many families with three and even four generations of rheumatic disease. Occurrence in a family, however, does not prove that it's inherited. The family could have been exposed to something in the environment that is the true cause. In Elizabeth's family, her maternal grandmother and aunt had severe crippling rheumatoid arthritis. Kathy had iritis a few years ago and now has recurrent joint pains.

Severe stress is another triggering factor at the onset of JRA. Severe stress can be caused by a divorce or separation of parents, a death of a family member, or adoption. Several studies report high frequencies of severe stress at the onset of JRA. Time after time, mothers of new JRA children told me about a recent divorce or separation. They would say, "It's almost like God was getting even," or "It came on too fast after the separation to be an accident."

Another striking association at the onset of JRA is severe injury. No one thinks that trauma causes JRA, but certainly injury can trigger a disease flare-up, including onset. A teenage boy who was a patient in our center developed arthritis after falling off a truck swinging around a corner. He did not break any bones but developed severe arthritis in virtually all joints at the moment of impact. His illness continued for several years.

Immunizations such as rubella or DTP produce an antibody response in the body and can precipitate the onset of a chronic arthritis that is indistinguishable from JRA. Indeed, many of us feel that infections such as flu, infectious mono, or Lyme disease cause a "reactive arthritis." This means that the body develops arthritis as a reaction to the illness much like serum sickness to chemicals such as penicillin. Children who develop this kind of arthritis usually have joint swelling for a short duration in terms of weeks. A few of these children can develop long-lasting arthritis. You will have to decide with your doctor whether your daughter or son should get the usual immunizations. To not give the immunizations runs the very real risk of getting such diseases as diphtheria, polio, or measles. On the other hand, to cause a flare-up of arthritis can be just as serious.

In terms of causes, you're going to hear from more than one friend or relative about a rheumatoid arthritis personality. Is there a JRA personality? For many years noted psychologists and rheumatologists wrote and worried about a "rheumatoid personality" predisposed to JRA. The personality characteristics described included depression, hostility, and difficulty in expressing anger. Controlled studies done in Houston comparing asthmatic with JRA children revealed no "rheumatoid" personality. The above observations relate to all children already afflicted with a painful, chronic illness. In other words, the "rheumatoid personality" is nonsense. So dump this one from your worry list along with strange and unconventional therapies.

Growth in Children with JRA

Sooner or later we need to talk about growth and whether it's affected by arthritis. Usually not, but it surely can be. The more severe the arthritis the more likely growth will be slowed in your child. There are several things you can do about a slow-down of growth—so pay attention! The main way that growth or weight is reduced is by poor appetite and inadequate food intake. Children feel terrible and just don't want anything to eat or drink. Some of the medicines reduce appetite or cause an upset stomach. With your team nutritionist (see Chapter 4) you can figure ways to increase dietary intake in your child.

The arthritis itself can slow total growth, and one of the medicines occasionally necessary, cortisone or a derivative, at times can stall growth in its tracks. Also, local stalling of growth in joints such as the jaw may occur, but there are ways to help these problems with surgery later.

About the time all of this starts to make a little sense, I have to tell you of something that sounds off-the-wall. Sometimes, one knee with arthritis grows too quickly, not too slowly. How about that! It can get to be an inch or so too long over the other knee. The reason is the arthritis causes too much blood to circulate to the affected knee to fight the inflammation. This causes the arthritic knee to grow faster than the normal knee. If it happens, there is something to do about it, but ultimately the knees will equalize most of the time. On unusual occasions a lift to the shoe of the short leg helps with walking. On rare occasions stapling the knee-growth center of the longer leg stops growth there and allows the short leg to catch up.

Onset of JRA

The onset of JRA—what happens in the beginning months of the disease—is a clue to which of the three major onset types of JRA your child has: pauciarticular JRA (four or fewer joints with arthritis), polyarticular JRA (five joints or more with arthritis) or systemic JRA (spiking fever and rheumatoid rash). There is also a small, maverick group of JRA children that don't quite fit anywhere. These are boys who have pauci JRA, usually with arthritis in the legs. They often have heel pain and inflammation of the heel tendons (tenosynovitis). These boys also are HLA-B27 positive. This is a genetic marker blood test that is associated with a related arthritis of the back. The reason for bringing it up is to let you know that our knowledge is imperfect and there are many "overlaps" in the rheumatic disease milieu. As arthritis progresses, one thing will look like another, and later on like yet another. So if your doctor says that your child is changing from one type to another, or seems to have symptoms of some other rheumatic disease, don't look to the ceiling and mumble, "Here we go again."

Pauciarticular Onset JRA *(Four Joints or Fewer)*

If you must have JRA, this is the one to have. About 45 percent have pauciarticular JRA. Children with this type have very few joints swollen, usually in the legs. Pauciarticular JRAs are usually girls younger than 10 years.

An example is Mary, a five-year-old kindergarten student who notices a little pain and discomfort in the knee off and on for several weeks or even months. Her mother one day notices a little swelling in the knee and sees that Mary can no longer straighten it. In a week or two she notices that one or two other joints are swollen. In the mornings her leg is stiff for about an hour after getting up.

While her arthritis is mild, there is a glitch. When they visit the eye doctor he finds local inflammation of the eye (iritis). It is mild, and prompt treatment controls it. Only 5 to 10 percent of all children with JRA ever develop iritis but most of them are in the pauciarticular group, and almost all are girls.

Progress of Pauciarticular JRA

Watching the progress of pauciarticular JRA would be like standing still and looking at one or two swollen joints in the knees or ankles as they got better or worse for months or years. The majority of pauciarticular JRAs have no sign of swollen joints in a few years. Quite a few of the rest do become polyarticular JRA with more than four joints involved, and only a few hang in there with a knee or hip for years and years. We'll talk more about them later. Here is where treatment with physical therapy and medicines will make a big difference in being able to use legs and arms normally later. Even though only one or two joints are swollen or limited in motion, losing good use through weakness or restricted motion in a knee or ankle is just as bad as having many joints swollen. So don't let this get ahead of you if you can help it.

Something you need to observe because you can do something about it is weakness of the muscles in the leg or arm around a joint with arthritis. This probably causes more of a mess than almost anything. In Mary's arthritis of the knee, the pain caused a limp. Because of the limp she used that leg less, so the calf and thigh muscles became smaller, which weakened that leg. This caused too much stress and strain on the good leg, and excessive use of the normal leg produced its own arthritis. What you can do is work with the physical therapy program described in Chapter 5 to prevent the loss of strength.

During the progress of pauci JRA or for that matter, polyarticular JRA, a low-grade fever occurs that is more a nuisance than a problem. This fever is 102°F or less and tends to remain for hours at a time, particularly in the evening. Most children have fever from 99° to 101°. The low-grade fever is completely nonspecific and occurs in many chronic illnesses. Remember that unless fever is causing your child to feel awful, there's no need to treat it.

We need to spend a few minutes talking about the eye and the eye doctor. You as a parent usually cannot tell that iritis has occurred; it can be spotted by the eye doctor. Iritis usually lasts only a few weeks or months. Early treatment is excellent at alleviating the inflammation. Very few have serious visual difficulty later. While all children with JRA need to see the eye doctor regularly, children with pauci JRA need to go most often to be sure that iritis has not happened. It is very treatable by using eye drops that dilate the pupils and sometimes cortisone derivatives.

Outcome of Pauciarticular JRA

It's always nice to read neat percentages of how many do this or how many do that, but the bottom line for you is how your child will do. Most pauci JRA children remain with only one or two joints swollen, and after several years have no more trouble. Some children have no trouble after one or two years. They are the lucky ones who rarely have iritis. There are a few children who get a joint involved, and it lasts and lasts and lasts no matter what you do. Just be sure you and your child do your best to prevent loss of use or motion.

There are some who are not so lucky. They go on to have many joints involved and long-lasting disease. While our intent in this chapter and throughout the book is to stay away from doom and gloom—there's always enough of that to go around—you need to know that while the light at the end of the tunnel is NOT an oncoming train, it may take you and your child longer to reach the end than either of us hopes. Enough said.

Polyarticular Onset JRA *(Five Joints or More)*

Elizabeth's story in Chapter 1 says it all. While many children with polyarticular onset JRA fortunately do not suffer the pain she endured, the onset is something you remember always. It can be insidious, however, and creep up on you when you're not looking.

Perhaps one child in four has polyarticular JRA, or arthritis in five joints or more, within six months of the beginning. These children have swelling in many joints and worse disease. The vast majority are girls who are older than the children with pauciarticular or systemic onset.

Even though you're not going to be on the edge of the chair with this next sign and a barn-burner issue this is not, you need to know about it anyway. Many, but not all, of the poly JRA children have what we call rheumatoid factor in their blood. They are RF positive. RF is a special antibody related to the gamma globulin proteins which is positive in almost all adults with rheumatoid arthritis. A raging controversy in the medicine men's lodge is whether this test is the real thing and the ultimate diagnosis of JRA. Don't lose any sleep over it, but at least you know about it.

Children with polyarticular JRA, many with a positive rheumatoid factor, often have enlargement of lymph nodes (kernels under the arms, for example) and develop lumps under the skin called subcutaneous nodules. Like the fever and rash, nodules under the skin are a little unsettling but cause no harm. The movable lumps under the skin are not painful and are usually located around the elbows, wrists, forearms, shins, ankles, or feet, attached to the covering of the bones or other deep tissue. They are harmless, appearing and disappearing, and usually last for no more than a few months. In my experience, patients with these nodules have more trouble with their arthritis later. The liver may be slightly enlarged but causes no problems. Anemia can be a nuisance. The low-grade fever discussed in pauci JRA occurs in poly JRA also. This is the most potentially destructive type to the joints, and one where we really push active and aggressive treatment with medicines and physical therapy.

Progression of Polyarticular JRA

The majority of children with poly JRA continue to have inflammation in many joints. A few have a reduction in the number of inflamed joints to two or three. Poly JRAs are the ones most likely to have serious injury to the cartilage and bone of the joints. They also are more likely to have loss of motion in joints. Kids in this group need the most aggressive treatment with the second line medicines discussed in Chapter 6. They also are more likely to have a change in life-style because of the physical disability. So what does this mean to you? It means that you're going to work harder earlier with physical therapy and all of the other things we'll talk about. It means that you won't wait for disaster to happen—you'll be ahead of the game.

Outcome of Polyarticular JRA

Poly JRA kids are more likely to have some functional loss of motion of the joints. Hard work to minimize this is your new watchword. They also are the ones most likely to go on to adulthood with arthritis, but again, most of this group grow up, get a job, marry, and live in a separate place from Mom and Dad.

Systemic Onset JRA

Explosive is the best way to describe the beginning of systemic JRA. Six-year-old Cindy awakens at night burning up with 105° fever. Horrified, her mother sees a splotchy rash on the girl's body and face which is salmon-pink and comes and goes. Every joint in her body is painful and swollen. She cries and cries asking for help to make the pain go away.

Attention is total and immediate. Hospitalization is frequent at this early stage. Infections begin in a similar way and many tests are done to look for other diseases. As time passes the special JRA rash and spiking fever lasting a few hours once or twice a day tell the story. The arthritis continues.

Other organs in the body are affected. The sac around the heart fills with fluid and can cause problems for Cindy. The liver, spleen, and lymph nodes enlarge. Even the kidneys do not escape unscathed and blood cells are found in the urine. Serious anemia shows up and causes Cindy to tire easily. The white blood cells are markedly increased in the blood count, causing further concern about infection.

About 30 percent of children with JRA are systemic onset. It's an equal opportunity condition—boys are affected in the same numbers as girls.

We need to spend a few minutes talking about the special fever of JRA. It is called intermittent or spiking fever and is greater than 103° and often 105°, lasting a few hours in the evening before returning to normal. One or even two episodes occur each day. During the spikes of fever Cindy usually feels terrible, or at least much worse than usual. The spiking fever resembles the fever that occurs in other diseases such as serious infections. For this reason exhaustive tests are needed at times to rule out infection if the characteristic rash is absent.

The other major feature of systemic JRA is the rheumatoid rash, which usually accompanies the JRA fever. It is one of the strangest things you'll ever see. Brothers and sisters will sit, and sit some more, to watch it move around the body every few minutes. Many types of rashes, from hives to measles, occur in children. Many strange and unknown rashes also occur in children with JRA. There is, however, a specific and characteristic rash in children with systemic onset JRA. It is salmon-pink and smooth with clearly defined, irregular borders, varying in size from a small button to several inches in diameter, with a pale center. Located anywhere on the body but most often on the trunk and face, it moves around and comes and goes in minutes. Occasionally the rash itches and rarely is raised. It is considered a vascular rash and in itself is not injurious to the body.

A less obvious problem is fluid around the heart, or more accurately the sac around the heart. No symptoms or discomfort to your child are present, and usually an ultrasound test, the echocardiogram, is needed to detect this fluid. It is mainly useful as a diagnostic test for systemic JRA. Unless your child has symptoms such as shortness of breath or chest pain, or your doctor hears a rubbing sound over the heart with the stethoscope, don't give the heart a second thought.

Even if pericarditis (that's what it's called) happens—it is rarely life-threatening, usually lasts a few weeks or months, and is treatable.

Progression of Systemic JRA

The good news is that the JRA fever and rheumatoid rash episodes of a few weeks or months disappear after five years and often before that. Other than being a pain in the you-know-what, no injury is done to the body. The episodes of fever come and go with flares of the arthritis. An infection such as a sore throat can set off the fever and rash along with the arthritis. The episodes usually last a few weeks, and the medicines we use are particularly helpful to control the fever. The longest-lasting systemic JRA fever in my practice was almost eight years with no remission. Several children in my practice had flare-ups of spiking fever and arthritis 10 and 20 years after we thought they were in remission.

All of the children in this group also join the pauci or the poly JRAs. The children who only have one or two joints with active arthritis have it made. They must be sure to prevent as much loss of motion and strength as possible with the programs we'll be discussing with you, but on the whole they'll be in good shape. Remember, however, that even though only one joint is afflicted, great injury can occur. It does NOT follow that one joint means that the JRA process won't injure that joint because it is so mild. Children with many swollen joints at times have no signs of permanent injury. The key is a regular physical therapy program.

The kids who follow a course of more than four arthritic joints or a poly course have more chances of loss of function and injury to the joints. If your child is in this group, both of you will have to be enthusiastic in following the program.

The other organs that may be enlarged such as the liver, spleen, and lymph nodes do not produce any serious injury by themselves. Pericarditis (inflammation of the sac around the heart) can cause problems, but the inflammation is not permanent nor does it leave any permanent damage.

Outcome of Systemic JRA

As I said, the terrible fever and nuisance rash go away, and the heart almost never becomes a permanent problem even if you have pericarditis. Death in JRA is about one percent and is usually due to heart disease, infection, or an adverse reaction from a medicine. If you're lucky in the draw and have only one or two inflamed joints, your course will be like pauci JRA with little risk of iritis. If you have many joints involved, you'll have to work doubly hard because you do have a greater risk of damage to the bone and cartilage of the joints and loss of normal use.

Ruling Out Other Diseases

As you remember, at the onset of your child's JRA, the doctors were probably puzzled and in a quandary as to just what she had. Some of these other conditions are "rheumatic"—related to arthritis. Indeed, some are so similar in symptoms that they overlap. Remember we talked about the maverick group of boys who are HLA-B27 positive? As an example, polymyositis causes inflammation of the muscles, pain, and weakness; so can JRA at times. Another thing you're going to hear about ad nauseam is the ANA, or antinuclear antibody test. This is a blood test that is positive in several of the rheumatic diseases, including JRA. Its chief value is to rule out lupus or SLE where it is present in large amounts.

Lupus-SLE—that's the ANA one—causes arthritis very similar to JRA at times. Acute rheumatic fever causes heart problems which can be difficult to distinguish from JRA. Even more, I have seen children change from one to the other. This does not mean an error was made. It's just how it is.

Stiffness in the Mornings

One of the many unexplained things in JRA is the inactivity stiffness of muscles and tendons. After sitting for an hour or so or sleeping all night, children with morning or inactivity stiffness tell you that they have trouble moving or "getting going." It is more than pain, although pain may be present also. It is different from weakness. Most children describe it as an inability to move the muscles. As they move around for a while, the difficulty getting up or walking disappears or becomes much better. Inactivity stiffness lasts from a few minutes to all day and is one of our main targets for treatment because when severe, it greatly restricts the life-style of your child.

Yes! The weather or infections can make the joints worse.

A lot of kids with arthritis really can tell when the weather is going to change for the worse with cold, wet, and miserable days ahead. They can tell because morning stiffness hits them a lick, and joint pain and swelling flare. The warning flare-up may come a day or two before the change, the same day, or a day or so later.

Why does this happen? Studies of adults in controlled-environment rooms show that when the barometric pressure is decreased rapidly and the humidity is increased quickly at the same time, the inflamed joints begin to hurt. When either the barometric pressure or humidity are changed separately, the pain does not occur. The phenomenon occurs with any joint injury or inflammation. It is not limited to JRA.

As an aside, the flare-ups of pain and swelling are not only influenced by the weather. Almost any infection can flare the arthritis. Upper respiratory infections are the most common in children and most flare-ups occur in this group. Diarrhea or any other infection can do it, however. You just have to see whether infection causes your child to get worse. If colds don't seem to matter one way or the other, don't sweat it.

Traveling Down the Road with Arthritis

You need to get a feeling for the ups and downs, as well as detours, ahead with regard to the joints and muscles. This will help you to understand why we go to such lengths to persuade you to be an aggressive team member with physical therapy, medicine, and other parts of the program. The good news is that after months or years of continual or intermittent swelling and pain, the joint disease in a particular joint "burns out" and active arthritis is gone. Different joints will be active or inactive at different times.

Pain is the single most important problem to address. It causes fatigue and irritability all by itself. Pain saps the strength of your child faster than anything else. At times children—and adults—have to learn to cope with unremitting pain and function in life, but we always keep trying to relieve it. The pain of arthritis in JRA is so variable that describing a pattern is difficult. Pain sometimes is worse in the morning after a night of rest, or attempted rest. Other times it's worse in the evenings after too much activity for that day. Then again the pain can last all day and night. Various treatments are directed at relief of pain as a number-one objective. These include not only medicines but heat, exercise, and of all things, water beds.

The muscles are involved in a passive way. They get weaker as they are used less because of pain in joints. They become stronger with active physical therapy. The size of the muscle fibers also becomes larger with use and smaller with disuse.

Sometimes you think it's just about over. The pain is gone; the swelling is so slight that you can barely see it, and then WHAMO! The weather changes or a bad bronchitis floors the child, and the pain and swelling return with a vengeance. Cheer up. It gets better. Physical therapy is so important here. It's tough to see that you're getting anywhere when the muscle size and strength only return to what they were before all that work. But when you see how weak the muscles are with no exercise and all that pain, your hard work and your child's hard work really make you feel good.

Joint motion depends on several factors. Pain hurts, and your child will favor the painful leg or arm. Spasms of muscles resulting from pain also reduce motion. When you touch the muscles under the skin, the child pulls away. The joint capsule can be so thickened that the scar tissue reduces motion. This is where treatment to reduce pain and swelling and improve motion is so important. Better muscular strength and endurance are essential.

Let's impose on our orthopedist, Dr. Malcom Granberry, and sneak into his operating room to look at a joint through the arthroscope. The arthroscope is a medical magnifying glass tube that allows us to look inside the knee joint of someone with JRA. What you see is that the swelling you feel is actually inside the capsule of a knee. The capsule is actually a casing or envelope enclosing the knee joint, including the knee cap. The swollen knee feels thickened, soft, and boggy. The inflamed tissue and fluid inside the capsule cause the swelling of the knee. The capsule is also thickened, as are tissues under the skin at times. The swelling looks as if it ought to hurt tremendously, but many times, surprisingly little pain is present. Even when pain is not a complaint, the body always protects itself and loses motion and strength, unconsciously reducing joint motion.

A second kind of joint swelling requires early, active physical therapy and relief of pain. There is rapid onset of extreme pain and tenderness in a joint accompanied by serious loss of motion. Early treatment with all of the stops pulled out is called for here. This type, in my experience, most often goes along with progressive destructive arthritis and loss of motion. There is little swelling present, and the fingers and wrist are a frequent site. Elizabeth's arthritis was an example of this type.

The soft tissue swelling eventually disappears. Three children out of four will have no injurious destruction of bone or cartilage. Permanent injury, if it occurs, is related to scar tissue and contraction of tendons or excessive thickening of joint capsules in such important joints as knees, hips, wrists, or fingers. Unfortunately, the bones and cartilage do not escape injury. About one child in four will have what we call erosive arthritis of bone or injury to the growth cartilage. Fortunately, very few children have injury sufficient to require surgery. At the present time the medicines that we use do not prevent erosive arthritis, but we hope that some at least reduce the destruction. I personally believe that our long-term use of the nonsteroidal drugs discussed in Chapter 6 has reduced the number of children with such severe disease.

To help understand why active exercise and medicines to relieve pain in joints are so important from the beginning, let's discuss what pain alone and arthritis also do to the mechanics of the body.

Even though Mary only has a knee involved with arthritis, the effects on her life are disproportionately greater. She limps because of the pain and uses that leg less. The calf and thigh muscles become smaller, which weakens the painful leg and causes too much strain on the good leg. Excessive use of the normal leg then produces its own trauma and arthritis.

In the hand and wrist area, reduced movement of the fingers and wrist impairs the ability of a child to write and grasp objects. In the back of the neck, arthritis causes loss of motion. This sets up a chain reaction that causes the head to be held with the chin jutting out, and leads to bad jaw motion and function. It also forces your child to move the entire body to look to the right or left.

Once again, enough said. You can see how important it is to stay on top of getting better.

Grown-Up Children with JRA

Interestingly, children who receive coordinated care at pediatric rheumatology centers for many years achieve higher educational levels than the normal population. At one center, more than 8 of 10 JRA patients were employed or in school after reaching adulthood, and 8 of 10 were married. So you and your child can look forward to a fulfilling life.

Preliminary information from a study in Washington, D.C. reveals that many teenagers with serious JRA are not prepared emotionally for job placement. There seems to be a mind-set of limited expectations built in for years by the attitudes of others. It may relate to doctors, parents, and teachers who somehow do not expect much achievement from chronically ill children and teenagers. So this is an area where you can make sure that your child is prepared and has good self-esteem. Expect something from your child from this moment on, if you don't already.

To close this chapter I'd like to share with you a holiday card from a former patient, Angela Withers, now a physical therapist. Angela had such severe arthritis for years that she missed school for weeks or months on end and often could not rise from her bed.

Dr. Brewer,

Hi! I hope you are doing fine and that you are enjoying the holiday season. I talked with your physical therapist at a physical therapy job fair earlier this year, and she caught me up on you. It sounds like you have been very busy.

I wanted to write you and tell you how well I have been doing. I see my new doctor and he has me on the same Rx that you started me on six years ago. Every year I seem to do better. I have been working at a physical therapy service for the past three and one half years and I manage our aquatics/fitness program. I also work with the physically challenged through the school system. I love my job. Most of the time I feel pretty good. I even am very active—exercise 3–4 times per week: swimming, treadmill and weight lifting (Nautilus). I do a lot of manual therapy so my hands, wrists, and shoulders flare-up at times but my knees are really much better. I did have a second surgery—this time my right big toe with fusion and a screw at DIP. No problems since the surgery though.

I write all of this just to say THANK YOU because you are why I have done so well. You always motivated me and encouraged me to do everything that I could. You were always more than a doctor had to be and I will always remember you. Thanks for everything. Take care.

Merry Christmas!
Love,
Angela

Her words spring from the page showing a successful and vibrantly alive young woman who lives life to its fullest. She is successful personally and professionally and looks forward to each day. Angela contributes to the community with her service and cares for herself. I suggest that she is this way because of her earlier adversity and how she addressed it. Try to do the same for your child!

3

Stepping Off the Emotional Roller Coaster

As a mother, my emotional response to Elizabeth's arthritis overwhelmed me. The intensity of your own response will probably surprise you. Know that you are not alone. I have never heard a parent who did not express utter disbelief that this was happening to his or her child. Your feelings are completely normal. To know this won't necessarily help alleviate them but it may assure you to know that they are shared by every other parent facing a similar situation.

In the course of the last eight years, as a spokesperson for the American Juvenile Arthritis Organization, I have met many parents who were facing a future for their child that was infinitely less than they had anticipated. I watched as they struggled to accept a limited physical existence for their child and eventually accepted, or did not accept, that reality. The ones who realized the physical limitations imposed by the effects of arthritis had an enormous advantage over those who did not. The ones who did not accept the situation had limited options. Many of them created problems because of their denial. Earl and I know one young lady who is considerably impaired today, in great part because her father steadfastly refused to admit that she had arthritis. He refused to participate in her treatment or acknowledge her need for physical therapy or anything else related to arthritis. You cannot solve a problem unless you first admit that there is a problem.

But no matter how hard we try, no matter what sacrifices we

make, it may not be enough. Our child is in pain. And when we see our child in pain I think we all have the same emotional response. It is HORRIBLE. How we handle this emotional side of the equation will have far-reaching ramifications for the future of the entire family. We must get a firm grip on the psychological effects so that we don't let arthritis dominate the life of the family.

Of course the first priority is to educate ourselves about the disease and how to treat its symptoms. This can be extremely difficult, given the emotional roller coaster we are riding in the early days. There is so much mental anguish that it is difficult, if not impossible, to focus on what the health professionals are saying. And sometimes in our anger we fall into the old problem of "shooting the messenger," usually the physician. Family members frequently vent their anger against their doctor. I was so overwhelmed emotionally when Elizabeth was diagnosed that I had an extremely short fuse. And, of course, we usually lash out at the people closest to us. We need to be careful in these treacherous days not to damage important relationships, whether they are with the medical professionals, our family members, or our friends.

But as impossible as it seems, focus we must. The most important thing is to try to prevent permanent damage to your child's body. This is an all-encompassing project. It will consume many hours of your day, depending upon the severity of your child's arthritis. It is so easy to overlook the psychological needs of everyone involved while you adjust your life to an entirely new and often erratic schedule. To say that "life goes on" is a truism that certainly applies here. Your child's arthritis will run its course. Hopefully you can help create a successful ending. In the meantime you don't want to jeopardize your marriage, your relationship with your other children and family members, or your other friendships.

Look Outward

From a personal standpoint I probably did just about everything wrong on an emotional level when Elizabeth was first diagnosed. I did become very determined and was totally dedicated to helping her through that time, but I also turned totally inward.

For six months we really weren't sure what was going on with her medically. A few people, mostly physician friends, said really stupid, hurtful things to me. Some of them became overnight experts in juvenile rheumatic diseases. They were second guessing Earl, and they said things that sent me into orbit. They may have been talking abstractly, but they were talking about *my* daughter. Then I began to avoid my friends, thinking that they really didn't want to hear all the "bad news."

In my determination I was doing *everything* for Elizabeth. I became physically exhausted. I ceased doing all the activities I had previously enjoyed so much: I stopped playing tennis, working in the garden, seeing my friends. There was no leisure time.

Of course I considered it a trade-off: my life to keep my beautiful daughter whole. It seemed logical to me. But having the distance I now have from the problems I must tell you that a much healthier approach would be a more balanced one. I have just described a depressed person—perhaps not in the strict clinical sense, for I was not totally immobilized, but I was depressed. The worst thing I could have done was to give up the things which had always been "therapy" for me. It would have been much healthier to *make* time for that therapy.

I understood later that I had really underestimated my friends. I have several really incredible friends from my childhood in Houston. They are friends not only in prosperity but in adversity as well. I did not give them the chance to understand what we were going through. But you must communicate your needs before people can help. We all know who our friends are. I urge you to give them the opportunity to help. Just turn the script around. Would you not rush to help one of your friends? Most people want to help but don't even know how to ask the question. Give them the opportunity to help a friend.

I am probably the worst offender in this area. My most used expression growing up was, "Please, I would rather do it myself." I still find it very difficult to ask for help. I did not even ask my family members for help. It is with great embarrassment that I tell you this. But hindsight is wonderful. This attitude did create quite a few problems for me later, not the least of which were total physical fatigue, depression, anxiety, and a few others. In the course of a lifetime we all have many obligations that must be fulfilled. But a healthy person will find pleasurable activities to balance her life. I repeat, BALANCE!

Another good source of help is to contact other parents of children with arthritis, preferably those who have been fighting the battle for some time. They can be a tremendous source of information and comfort. And boy, do they know what your family is going through. Your doctor may be able to refer you to someone, or your local chapter of the Arthritis Foundation may know other families in your area.

Acceptance as a Beginning

With the distance in time from those days I can see the mistakes I made, but believe me, in the heat of battle you can become very myopic. Elizabeth was doing just fine. I was not. In five years she was beginning to recover from her arthritis and move on to the next phase of her life. I was not. It is ironic that it was something that Elizabeth said to me that began my journey back to a normal life.

At this time Earl had begun Elizabeth's gold injections again. Because of adverse reactions to the many drugs she had tried, we were literally running out of medications to control the symptoms. Even though Elizabeth had had a bad reaction to the gold injections earlier, she was now five years older and a few pounds heavier, and a decision was made to "rechallenge" her with the gold. As far as I'm concerned it was a desperation move. And we were desperate. Many people had told me that these injections were extremely painful. One woman said they were so painful that she decided she would rather cope with the pain of her arthritis than take them. Each time we went for the injection I carefully observed Elizabeth's reaction. She did not blink an eye. I would ask her if it hurt. She always brushed the question aside. One day after she had stoically taken her injection and we were waiting for the elevator outside Earl's office, I again asked her if the injection hurt. She paused for a moment, turned to me, and said, "Don't you understand, Mom? I have been through so much with my arthritis, this is just something else that I have to get through. What is pain for other people is different for me. I have accepted it. I have other things I want to do. I have to get on with my life. I don't have time for this."

Could a psychiatrist have said it better? This child had just given me the best prescription possible. Some pain will never go away. It will not subside. I can either accept it, incorporate it into my life and continue living, or it will destroy me. It is really quite simple. It is a choice. From that day I chose to accept the pain, as Elizabeth had done, and get on with my life.

Exercise and Hobbies as Therapy

Having a child with a chronic disease is very much like losing a child. One day you have a perfect child and the next you have a less-than-perfect child. Many parents are unable to accept that fact. For every parent going through the enormous stress of seeing your child ill, I would urge you to examine your life prior to the onset of the disease and remember what you enjoyed doing. What activities helped you forget your daily cares? Are you getting enough exercise?

We make clear the importance of physical therapy for your child with arthritis. But physical therapy is nothing more than being physically fit. We all need to be physically fit to really enjoy life. If you realize that you have given up a much-enjoyed activity you really should examine why. See if you can resume this activity with the help of family or friends. There are times when we simply must be kind to ourselves.

I wish someone had given me that simple advice.

Creatively Eliminating the Nemesis

Another way I have managed to put things in perspective in my life has been to put it down in writing. Psychologists are now exploring the fact that people who are able to write about a traumatic event in their lives may have better mental and physical health than those who cannot. When we are inundated by an overwhelming event, something over which we have little or no control, writing seems to allow us to organize our thoughts and express feelings we may have been previously suppressing. Once they are organized and recognized, hopefully we can then move on to resolve them. I have a friend in

Houston, an artist, who has been keeping daily journals for years. I have not been so disciplined, but I do tend to write when I am struggling with a problem. It does help me organize my thoughts, analyze my feelings, and generally bring a focus to my problems. I really feel that for some people writing can clarify their feelings. For me it helped a great deal.

I would not only encourage you to keep a journal, but I would definitely encourage your child to express her feelings in writing. I have read several poems written by children with arthritis. It seems to be a way for them to vent their anger, fear, and frustration. Or if they are too young to write, perhaps you can use art as a means of expression. Children express the most incredible depth of feeling through drawing when they really can't express their thoughts verbally. Many museums offer this type of art course for children. The teachers are trained to bring out a child's ability to express feelings through art. There are also books to show you how.

Photography is another thing that helped Elizabeth a great deal. We all need to feel that we have a talent, a unique ability. She had been so active before she became ill that she really needed to find outlets for all that energy. We set up a darkroom in a small bathroom. She became very creative with her pictures and eventually became a photographer for the school yearbook. Photography can be a relatively inexpensive hobby, especially nowadays, with all the places that have one-hour film development. And it is such fun to see your handiwork so quickly. Try it!

Regardless of what activity your child decides to pursue, don't forget to compliment all of her endeavors. We all need a pat on the back from time to time, some positive feedback, but especially if you are in the process of rearranging your life.

Faith and Humor as Antidote

The two things that helped me through this extremely difficult period were my faith in God and a sense of humor. I truly believe that things happen for a reason and everything in the universe is exactly as it should be. I accept that philosophy, for every trauma I have suffered in my life has been a stepping stone to a new plateau in my emotional and spiritual life. Whatever your faith or belief in a higher order, this is a time when you will need to draw strength from your beliefs. From my observations most parents initially believe that their child will have the worst possible effects from the arthritis. This is not usually the case. Be optimistic! Rely on your faith. *Believe* that your child *will* be better. It is very important to demonstrate that belief to your child constantly, and if your faith begins to waver, seek help from your clergyman. He has dedicated his life to helping people in a time of need.

Life is certainly difficult. One of Buddha's Four Noble Truths is that "life is suffering." But I have never been in a situation in which I could not look around me and find someone in a more difficult position than I was. The world is so full of pain and tragedy, you can always find a reason for gratitude if you really search your soul. Share it with your child. One such instance happened when we had to go to the hospital for an echocardiogram because Earl had discovered several heart murmurs. There were several other children going through the same procedure, children much younger than Elizabeth, all of whom had leukemia. Their hair had fallen out from the powerful chemicals used to treat their cancer. They were so frail, walking around with I.V.'s dripping fluids into their little bodies. It was a most sobering experience for both of us. Arthritis seemed somehow more manageable.

Now, finding humor in these situations is a little more difficult, but you must try. Realize that a Jim Henson I am not, but my hand puppets by the whirlpool seemed to entertain my daughter and lift her spirits—probably just the sheer absurdity of seeing Mom lying on the floor making an absolute fool of herself. Like Bob Hope, I'll do anything for a laugh! Laughter can certainly be a saving grace. This fact is finally being documented by the medical world—that laughter does indeed have all kinds of wonderful effects on our bodies. I think as a family you might consider adopting the motto, "Lighten Up!" I have a dear friend in Los Angeles, a young adult with arthritis who is now facing her fourteenth surgery for joint replacement. Instead of a "woe is me" attitude she went to the Department of Motor Vehicles and now has a car license plate that says "2 BIONIC."

Elizabeth's Perspective
(Or "My Mom the Psychologist")

When I told Elizabeth that I was writing this book she was excited. I let her read some of the preliminary drafts and she felt that it would be a great help for families to know that they are not alone. And maybe they could avoid some of the pitfalls we fell into. When I asked her what emotions she felt when we were going through those difficult times she spoke one word, *fear*; fear of what was happening to her body, fear of the future, fear of being so dependent on other people.

I remember one incident in the early days of her diagnosis. We were on one of our many doctor visits when she stopped, wrapped her arms around me, and said, sobbing, "What is happening to my body?" The only way to answer a question like that is with honesty. "I don't know. But we are in this together and we will find a solution together. And we will all be dependent upon another person at some time in our lives. How fortunate we are that we have people who love us and will help us through difficult times."

Many children have shared their feelings of wanting to just be "normal." Childhood is a time when we simply want to be like everyone else. It is sometimes difficult to convince children that they are not different when their lives are so upside down. Their classmates are not perpetually sitting in physicians' offices. They don't have to take medications constantly. They don't have to wear those awful splints. One thing we explained to Elizabeth was that these were temporary things that would enable her to be "normal" in the future, something she would have to tolerate in order to reach her goal. And keeping your eye on the goal is something we all need to do in our lives. But I also feel you should tell your child that it really is all right to be "different" sometimes. After all, we are each unique.

Another thought she shared with me was the tremendous sense of frustration she felt. She wanted Earl to give her some guarantee, to put some time limit on her illness, to tell her that she would be better within a certain time frame. He would not. Of course he *could not*. A child does not understand the vague nature of the illness. Children want to know when they will be able to go out and play with their friends again.

My father died of a heart attack at only 52 years of age when I was pregnant with Elizabeth. When she became really ill she frequently asked me how I had continued living when he died. She was very frightened of losing the people she had become so dependent upon.

Your child will need to be continually reassured that she is not alone, that she will be cared for, and that she will get better even though you cannot give her a specific time. It is a time of tremendous insecurity. I cannot stress enough the need to give your child the utmost support in these difficult days. The combination of chronic pain and fear has led more than a few children to contemplate suicide. Several adults who have had JRA and several parents of children with JRA have told me that, at times, suicide indeed had seemed to be a viable option. If you see your child withdrawing, or if you observe signs of depression, please seek professional help. Keep the lines of communication open between you and your child. Encourage your child to express her feelings, both positive and negative. Your ability as a psychologist will be tested to the limits.

Siblings

There are studies being done today that indicate that the siblings of children with arthritis are having more difficulty in later life than the children with arthritis. As a parent I have no problem understanding that concept. It requires an enormous amount of energy to keep your child with arthritis going. There are only so many hours in a day. Something or someone has to suffer the loss. In order to succeed in this effort you must devote enormous amounts of time and energy. It would be surprising if you did not have problems with your other children. Even if they understand at an intellectual level, they will have problems at an emotional level.

Brothers and sisters need to know what is happening medically. I really feel that ignorance breeds unnecessary fear. Let them know, in age-appropriate ways, just exactly what is happening to their sibling. Knowledge will only help them cope with the changes that may be occurring in their lives, as well.

Brothers and sisters will have to deal with all the same emotions you are facing, with the disadvantage that they are not usually involved in the educational process you are experiencing. Seeing someone they love in pain will cause them pain. They will probably feel very sad. And they may feel resentment, perhaps for all the attention the ill child is receiving. Many siblings have said they wanted to have arthritis, too.

When Elizabeth was diagnosed, Virginia was just beginning high school. Is there a more vulnerable time in your life? So at a time in her life when I should have been with her, sharing all her new adventures, advising her about all the new social situations, I was sitting in Earl's office, in the ophthalmologist's office, in the orthopedic surgeon's office, helping Elizabeth with therapy, taking her to be fitted with splints for her wrists, or going to a foot specialist to be fitted with special orthotic inserts to help her walk. All these projects, and many more, required an enormous amount of time, time away from the other children. Virginia tells me now that she understood the necessity of my attending to Elizabeth's problems. She was in so much pain and we all wanted to help her in every way possible. But if Virginia won't admit it, I will tell you that I feel the loss of those special times.

John and Virginia became actively involved with helping Elizabeth. They were truly remarkable, supporting her in so many ways, by administering physical therapy, by carrying her when she could not walk, by encouraging her when she was down, by sharing her pain. When we love a person, and that person is in pain, we also suffer. Selfishly we want to make that person better to alleviate our own pain. Sometimes people do and say strange things in their attempt to "make it better." How many times have you heard people say things like: "I'm really sorry that your mother died. I'm sure she's in heaven and better off." Or: "I always feel better if I go jogging." These are not always helpful things to hear. Often the only thing we can really do to help is just share the other person's pain. Just be with her, hold her hand, hug her. When Elizabeth was really ill, I used to sit in the bed with her and gently rub her swollen, inflamed joints. I did not tell her that I was silently praying that her pain could be transferred into my body. Many years later she recalled the episode and told me that she felt so much better when I rubbed her joints. Maybe miracles *do* happen.

For John and Virginia, I think being involved with helping Elizabeth helped them more. Teenagers tend to be very self-centered. These two had to learn early the importance of interdependence, of our essential interconnectedness. I think they grew as a result of these experiences.

One problem I have heard parents mention frequently is discipline. Chronically ill children can be extremely cantankerous. How do you discipline a child who is already in pain? John and Virginia handled it quite nicely, thank you. When Elizabeth was really impossible and demanding, they would put up with her behavior just so long. Then they would remind her that they were her main means of transportation. If she wanted to get somewhere she had better back off, period, end of discussion.

Even though it may be difficult at times, the best thing you can do for your child with arthritis is to treat her just like the rest of the group. Parents have to set limits for all their children or they will be trampled in the onslaught. Those limits are there for the sake of civilization and you should expect compliance from everyone. Common sense dictates that if we are all going to live in the same house we have to have mutual respect for one another.

A Father's Point of View

I obviously cannot speak from the father's point of view. I have, however, listened to and observed fathers for the past few years. There is a phrase that is currently popular in government and business that I think sums up what I have been hearing: "He was out of the loop." That describes the situation in which many fathers find themselves. They are usually so busy earning a living that they don't actively participate in the care of the child. Sometimes they are unable to, but often they are really denying the whole situation. I have seen this behavior more often than I would like to admit: the "Ostrich Syndrome."

When a child is diagnosed with arthritis, it is usually a young family. The father, and sometimes the mother, are beginning their careers and they are not usually in the best financial shape. It is a time when most people are beginning to invest and plan for the future. All those lab tests and doctor visits Earl refers to in Chapter 2 are very costly. If their child is uninsured the situation is disastrous. And if the father is with a firm that has insurance he will find it difficult to change jobs, no matter what his personal feelings, because of the difficulty of insuring a child with a "preexisting condition." The cost of caring for a chronically ill child may jeopardize future plans. The father finds he is under tremendously increased pressure to produce more income to cover all these costs. This is a recipe for serious problems.

Historically, men have not been given permission to express their deepest feelings. No parent could see her child in pain and not feel enormous pain herself. I cried a lot. Elizabeth's father did not, but I know he suffered as much as I did. I would encourage every father to become involved in the treatment of his child. Go to the doctor whenever possible. Try to understand the disease process. Help with physical therapy and medications. I think that active participation is one way to work through the grief you naturally must feel.

Grandparents

One group I have neglected to write about is grandparents. And one reason is because I have heard such tremendously different anecdotes about how they react to the news of their grandchildren developing this old person's disease. I know my own mother had a very difficult time seeing Elizabeth in such pain. Her visits became farther apart depending on just how ill Elizabeth was.

A father whose daughter is in college and has serious impairments because of the arthritis she has had most of her life tells an interesting tale of his parents. It seems they consistently deny that their grand-daughter has a problem, even to the extent that they send her totally inappropriate gifts. For example, she has limited use of her hands, and they will send a gift that requires considerable manual dexterity. I presume this is a way of coping with a problem that they simply can-not face. They deny that it exists, and in their world it doesn't.

At the other extreme, Dr. Balu Athreya of Philadelphia, one of the most conscientious physicians I have met, tells the story of a little patient who was having an extremely difficult time. She had a very difficult rheumatic disease. None of the medications were having any effect and the child continued to deteriorate despite his most dogged attempts to help. Day after day the little girl simply did not do well. He was at his wit's end, spending sleepless nights and consulting with many other colleagues. He did not know what to do next and he was afraid they might lose the child. Medical science had reached its limit.

But then he began to observe that every day the little girl's grandfather was at her bedside, telling her stories, gently brushing her hair, holding her hands as she slept, reading stories to cheer her. His love seemed to fill the room despite the pain he obviously felt seeing his granddaughter in this condition. No matter what the weather, he was there every day. Then slowly, for no apparent reason related to the medical treatment, the child began to show improvement. Balu will tell you that he does believe that the love and support this man displayed had a greater impact on the child than the efforts of medical science. Love is a tremendous power, and the love of a grandparent is a very special thing.

One thing many families have done is to bring the grandparents to the annual American Juvenile Arthritis Organization (AJAO) meeting. By comparing experiences with others, I have seen people transformed from total denial to total involvement. On a personal level, we might neglect to involve our parents in the educational process, and they are overwhelmed with fear for the future of their grandchildren. We really need to be aware of their need to understand exactly what is happening and that there are solutions they can certainly help with.

Organize That Chaos

One important aspect of all this is to try to maintain some semblance of sanity within the family. Your life is upside down. I cannot phrase it any other way. UPSIDE DOWN. Doctor's offices, laboratory tests, therapy, medicines, X-rays, splints, and so on. I kept hoping that I would wake up from the nightmare. After a while you really need a break.

I want to encourage you to have "normal" vacations with your family. Whether you have one child or eight, you need to create these memories for your children. A child diagnosed with arthritis feels tremendously guilty about depriving the rest of the family of "normal" times. I don't care how complicated the scene, please try to have these regular vacation times with your family. You will need to be aware of medications, rest, local medical resources, and the availability of flights to return home if necessary. (You don't want to be on a desert island!)

On a trip to South America to visit the family, Elizabeth insisted on carrying her own medication in her bag, the thesis being that she was a "big girl" and could manage her own things. That bag and her medication are probably in Fiji or Bora Bora now. I agree that you need to give your child responsibility. But I also did not want to have to fly all the way back to the States for medication. She could not function without her medicine and I knew that the prescription was unavailable in South America. I quietly carried extra medicine in case she forgot it. No, we did not have to return home. The vacation was saved because Mom had backups. Be prepared!

If your child is too ill to travel, or if it is just impossible for whatever reason, you can create a "stay at home" vacation. Set aside a block of time in which to do some of the fun things you would not ordinarily do. Go to the zoo, to the theater, to the museums in your area. Take day trips to nearby places, or have a picnic in the park.

If you are married, you should make it a priority to have time alone with your spouse. The divorce rate is higher in families of children with chronic illnesses. You need to carefully examine the kinds of stresses that are being put on your marriage. Because there seems to be a genetic component to many types of arthritis, the parent who has a family history of arthritis may feel tremendous guilt. I certainly did. The other parent may make insensitive reference to that fact, either privately or publicly. If remarks of this type are made, bring it up for discussion immediately. If you keep it inside it will just become distorted. Let the other person know how you feel. Those remarks are usually made without thinking, but you certainly don't want them repeated.

Another stress is the division of labor. Since the mother is usually the main caregiver she may feel that the father is not helping enough. She may not understand the added financial burden her husband feels. She may resent the extra time he spends at work. She feels he is escaping. He feels she has no understanding of the financial situation. Please set aside time alone to *communicate*. Try to keep it positive and not critical. Instead of, "Why aren't you here more?," make it, "I really need your help!" Together, with good will, you can work toward solutions. Be aware and be careful. It is a volatile time. The suppressed anger over your child's illness makes for a very short fuse. And unfortunately we tend to take it out on those closest to us. If you see problems that you cannot resolve, please get professional help.

Reach Out and Touch Someone!

Last, but by no means least, I would encourage you to look for a support group. The AJAO has actively encouraged the formation of support groups in the past 10 years. The Arthritis Foundation has chapters in most of the major cities and branches in many others. Call them to see if there are other families in your area who have children with arthritis. If there is no support group, start one. If your child is being treated by a pediatric rheumatologist, this professional may be able to guide you to other parents who are facing similar problems. No one will understand more than another family who has been down the same road. If they have been fighting the battle for some time they can probably give you some very helpful hints on survival techniques.

I guess what I am trying to say in this chapter is that you first need to accept all the anger, rage, and frustration you must feel over your child's illness. Then harness it and turn it into positive, creative, dynamic energy. Then use that energy to improve the quality of life for your child, for your family, and for yourself. These are the times that will bring forth all your strengths and expose your weaknesses. Appreciate your strengths, pat yourself on the back, and work like crazy to improve your shortcomings. And know that you are not alone.

4

A New Breed
of Health Professionals:
The Team Approach

*Each patient carries his own doctor inside him. . . . We
are at our best when we give the doctor who resides
within each patient a chance to work.*

—ALBERT SCHWEITZER

Arthritis impacts just about every facet of your child's life, as well as
yours and your family's. One of the first and most obvious facts you
will become aware of is that YOU NEED HELP. The concept of a
"health care team" has evolved because of the very real need for comprehensive, coordinated care for the child. Today's physicians do not
just treat the arthritis. They treat the child—the whole child.

After you recover from the news that your child has arthritis, a
first priority is to find the right medical care. (See Appendixes A and
B.) Since arthritis is a chronic condition, which means this is going to
be an ongoing relationship for your child, it becomes essential that you
find a physician you can relate to on *many* levels—someone like Earl. A
pediatric rheumatologist is, as the name implies, a pediatrician and a
rheumatologist. The specialty is a very young one. Today, it is where
pediatric cardiology was 20 years ago.

Children are not simply miniature adults. Their needs are dramatically different from those of adults. You need a specialist and a group of health care providers who understand all the ramifications of the medicines, their impact on the health and growth of the child, and someone who will help educate you and your family to ensure the best possible result. The one thing we all need is vast quantities of *information.* (See Appendix C)

Years ago, children with rheumatic diseases frequently spent long periods in the hospital. Fortunately today, doctors do everything possible to keep children out of the hospital setting. It's always better to have your child at home if possible. However, this does increase the need for the family to perform many functions. This is why the new breed of health professionals providing team care becomes so important. You and the team are co-captains in the care of your child and family.

Choosing the Right Doctor

Earl told me one time that for a doctor to be successful and well liked, he or she must be conscientious, available, really nice to people, and above all able to communicate. If he's super smart, that's nice but not essential. In order to educate a person you must necessarily be able to communicate effectively. If you feel you cannot talk to a doctor, start looking for a different one. If you are afraid to ask a question, any question, look for the door. All the knowledge in the world is not going to help if it cannot be imparted in a practical, useful manner. There must also be mutual respect. The physician may have a wealth of knowledge about the disease, but you certainly have a comparable amount of knowledge about your child.

There is often a tremendous anger directed at the physician by patients and families who feel they have been misunderstood. I attended a conference for parents of children with chronic illnesses in which parents were expressing their anger toward physicians. In my ignorance, and with a cheerful smile, I told them how happy I was with the way Earl was treating my daughter. They looked at me as if I were a pariah. It took me a while to grasp what these families had been going through. We had the good fortune to have a caring doctor for our daughter. Many of these parents had been treated with considerable disdain by their children's doctors. Many were afraid to ask even the most basic questions.

One of the main reasons my friendship with Earl Brewer has survived through a very difficult time is because of the way he dealt with my daughter. I must tell you that he treated her with the utmost respect. She was a very petite 11-year-old, he was a world recognized physician and teacher, over six feet tall. Their relationship was interesting, to say the least. It was definitely one of mutual respect. He respected the fact that she was in severe pain, in an alien world. She respected his credentials, but she demanded that he respect her as a person.

Elizabeth and I spent many, many hours sitting in waiting rooms, either for the lab tests or a doctor's appointment. We met several young adults with arthritis who had received large doses of steroids before scientists understood their impact on children's growth. Many of these young adults were not as large as 11-year-old Elizabeth. Many of them were severely disabled. It frightened her, and her question to me was, "Will I be like that?" Elizabeth was well aware of what over prescribing steroids in the past had done to many children. When steroids were first discovered, medical science thought they were the "miracle cure" for rheumatic diseases. But when prescribed in large doses they did really dreadful things to children's growth patterns. When Earl wanted to prescribe them for Elizabeth to try to bring her disease under control, her response was, "Not on your life!" His response was, "OK, Elizabeth, I respect the fact that you are frightened, and we are dealing with your body. We will work around steroids as long as possible. But there may come a time when we will have to prescribe steroids. You have to understand that steroids are a chemical naturally created in the body. We simply increase the dosage. We know today how to handle the levels of steroids better without doing serious damage to your body. We have learned to control the amount we give to children. But I respect your judgment."

I urge you to listen to how a doctor communicates with your child. Another doctor might have gone on and prescribed the steroids, not respecting the very real fear Elizabeth had. I can assure you that in her mental state anything could have happened if she had been forced to take them at that point.

Not everything went swimmingly with Earl. I will give you an example, if you won't tell him. Elizabeth's father had seen an article about a new medication in one of the journals, and he insisted that Earl try it on Elizabeth. (It must be awful for a doctor treating another doctor's child.) When I gave Earl the message, I could tell that he was not nearly so enthusiastic about the new medicine. Grudgingly he took out his prescription pad, and while writing the prescription he commented (in front of Elizabeth), "She'll probably throw up at about 3:00 A.M." I am here to tell you that she did exactly what the doctor said. She threw up at 3:00 A.M.

I felt like strangling both physicians. With this true story, I just wanted to illustrate how very great an impact our attitudes will have on a child. So choose your physician carefully.

Our Personal Cheerleader

The physician will have to refer you to other specialists for various medical reasons. He is the captain of the health team for your family, the coordinator for this very elaborate health care network. He must also take responsibility for seeing that all the information is processed properly and your child is *always* the main consideration.

The second part of finding the proper care is to be sure that the doctor you choose has a health team to back him up. Learning about the disease is like learning a new language. There will be many things the doctor will say that you simply do not understand. You may be home before you realize that it went completely over your head. The team nurse usually can answer your questions. In fact, she will probably be in charge of your JRA teaching course. In order to fully understand what is happening to your child, you will have to learn about medicines, physical therapy, occupational therapy, nutrition, psychology, orthopedic problems, eye problems, emotional problems, educational rights, and probably a few more topics. You will learn all of this while in a very emotional state—if you are the typical parent.

In the early months after the diagnosis, you will need a crash course in survival. I guarantee that you will not remember everything you hear the first time around. You will need a well-trained support team to guide you through the maze and answer your many questions. A good pediatric rheumatologist will have health care professionals to lead, educate, and encourage you. He will also have printed materials for your use at home. Reading in the quiet of your own home really reinforces your learning. (See Appendix C)

In the appendixes we have included a fairly comprehensive list of pediatric rheumatologists and pediatric rheumatology centers. In my capacity as President of the American Juvenile Arthritis Organization, I had the pleasure of working with many of these physicians. I have been consistently impressed with their kindness, dedication, and determination to improve the quality of life for children with rheumatic diseases.

We definitely do not live in a vacuum. We are not isolated on an island. We are social creatures. We need each other. When we are in a state of crisis, we *really* need each other. I cannot imagine how a family can cope with a serious chronic illness without the aid of others in the community. Be diligent in your search for the proper team to help you and your child. In this age, we are all very "consumer" oriented, and you will definitely be paying for proper care. Don't be shy. Demand the very best for your child.

That said, I now relinquish the floor to Earl, who will be your guide to the team approach.

The Team Approach

Many of us long for the old days of Norman Rockwell with a family doc sitting at the bedside stroking his chin. Indeed, in the late 1950s I spent several years practicing pediatrics in Wharton, a wonderful small town of about 5,000 near Houston. I enjoyed the fulfillment of being a town doc making house calls and being a local authority on medicine and life in general. I wasn't even dry behind the ears yet.

Fortunately or unfortunately, those days are gone forever. The nostalgia is fun, but the reality is that medical skills have long since exceeded the ability of a single doctor or any other health professional to be all things to all people. Actually, a new breed of health professional is developing. The new kids on the block know that expert knowledge is spread around to a lot of people, and the trick for parents and the family physician is to intelligently and efficiently tap the knowledge of many people and services to provide the best care for the child with arthritis. Because so many services and people are necessary for the best care and diagnosis of arthritis, someone has to corral these fragmented pieces together so that they work. Another term for this is *coordinated care*. Where do you find this? At a pediatric rheumatology center. We must make these services available as close to the families' homes and as accessible as possible. We call them "community-based services." (See Appendix B.)

Some doctors and medical centers have somehow lost the point of care along the way. Caring for sick children and their families is a privilege. The medical center and the doctors are not the center of the universe, and they must not require families to revolve around their schedules. Their rationale has been that the center's space and time are so valuable that it is better for the patients to wait and wait and be inconvenienced rather than the team players. If you encounter this mistaken attitude, move on to another place of care. Life is too short to argue about it. Having said that, I must confess that I have kept patients waiting too long, usually because I would get so involved helping a family that the time would slip away from me. Excuses, excuses, but I know that I'll hear from a lot of people on this.

Even more important, the parents and the rheumatology care team must be partners in care. This includes decision making. Issues of concern here include the doc who says, "Of course I have a partnership with my families. I tell 'em what to do, and they do it." As with the "significant" or "indispensable others" in your life, you will quickly find out whether the doctor and team players treat you as a partner in care and practice "family-centered care." If they don't, find someplace else.

The Team Players

What about this team? Who are they? You say, "All I need is a gang of people hanging over my child, asking dumb questions while I wait to see the doctor." Wrong! The team is headed by the doctor. He is helped by a nurse, patient/family educator, nutritionist, social worker or equivalent, and physical therapist/occupational therapist. The core team works together so closely that they practice what I call "transdisciplinary care." Boy, is that a mouthful. The total of transdisciplinary care is greater than the sum of its parts. What that means is that each member of the team has skills not possessed by the others. By working together closely to solve your child's problems, they learn one another's basic skills so well that they can spot when a particular team member is needed for a particular problem and act accordingly. For example, after a while the educator can discuss basic normal nutrition as well as the nutritionist can.

The core team does not know everything either. They have a much larger consulting team whose services are needed for special situations that don't happen very often, such as eye problems. In fact you will not see all of the team members every visit. The larger consulting group consists of the eye doctor, orthopedic surgeon, psychologist, splint and brace person, special education specialist, and yes—a parent pal. We'll talk more about parent pals and special education specialists later.

Let's walk you through an imaginary first visit with the team so you get a feel for it.

Your pediatrician or orthopedist has said to you, "See the arthritis doctor." He calls for an appointment. You may get a questionnaire asking a lot of questions, or a phone call from the nurse or coordinator of the team. Fill out the questionnaire. It's not a waste of your time or a violation of privacy and will be useful to the team.

You may be seen first by the coordinator, or the nurse who will gather an early history helpful to the whole team including the doctor. Know that this person is just as important to helping your child and family as the doctor. Do not feel that your time is being wasted and ask to speak first to the doctor—the real reason for your visit.

The doctor you see will do the history and physical examination, discuss an early idea of what is going on, and give you a general plan for evaluating your child's and your family's needs. The nurse, who is often the coordinator, will make sure that the doctor's plan is put into effect. The various people you will see in addition to the pediatric rheumatologist and nurse, either that day or in a few days, are the physical therapist, social worker, educator, and nutritionist. I'm sure that an appointment will be made for your child to see the eye doctor.

The Nurse/Coordinator

The nurse is often the coordinator who makes it all happen. She shepherds you to the right places at the right time. She scurries around the clinic doing clinical things like taking blood pressures, drawing blood for tests, and scheduling appointments with other clinics. When the doctor speaks in rapid-fire lingo to no one in particular, she is the one who will interpret what "survey chem" and "the usual" mean to you; she will also put it on paper. Even better, she sees that it gets done. The team nurse also is the one whom you call with any and all problems and also is the one who will call others to find out answers to your questions. She is the best liaison to the doctor because she will call you back in a reasonable period of time. She's the one who runs interference when the eye doctor can't possibly see your girl for several months.

The Physical Therapist

The physical therapist will go over your child's joints and muscles to see how well they are working. A chart of involved joints and muscles probably will be completed. A functional assessment will be done that can be repeated as you go along to see how much improvement or loss of improvement occurs. *Functional assessment* is a formidable-sounding term that simply means what physical tasks your child can or cannot do. The assessment has been well standardized. You won't receive a planned exercise program until a diagnosis is made and the team decides on an overall strategy with you. You'll get pamphlets explaining an exercise program with specific exercises marked or written. Hopefully a general conditioning exercise program will be part of this plan.

The Social Worker

The social worker will get acquainted and offer services later as tough family situations crop up. The social worker also is a fount of information about these community-based services we've been so glibly talking about. These include the school services that will be so important to the future of your child. If you need to have a special, individual educational plan at school, the social worker will be the one to help—not only to arrange it but to coach you so you will perform well at the hearing. The social worker's information and referral knowledge also includes where to's and how to's—where to go for respite services (if they exist), how to apply for state aid after you've gone broke trying to pay for all of this, and where to find various medical and equipment services. Even more important, the social worker can steer you to a parent support group. I know, I know; you can solve your own problems, but it really helps if you can have a parent-pal who has been down the road to help you over the bad times. These kinds of programs are just getting started in Arthritis Foundation AJAO chapters. With a little luck your town will have one. If not, set up your own later. I bet that the team will help.

The Educator

The educator may be the nurse or a separate person. The educator is the key to success for the proper care of your child and must persuade you that the planned care program is not only proper but necessary—and that you will carry it out. This program is a mini-school for you and your child that involves talks and written material in planned segments. There will be pamphlets about JRA, and often you will be given selected pages from the Arthritis Foundation's *Understanding Arthritis*. Your center probably will have materials of its own. You can never read too much; also, you're going to forget most of it in a few weeks, so look at it again later. The educator will spend at least half an hour with you, talking one on one. Some centers use a video-tape about JRA prepared by Carol Lindsley, M.D. It's very good. The social worker may talk to you about social concerns. As you go along, the nurse will give you printouts about new medicines you are to receive. These sheets have a short discussion of the new medicine and how it hopefully will help. The possible adverse effects of the medicine are included.

An important part of the educator's function is to have the skill to educate both you and your child, and don't forget the brothers and sisters; they're in this thing, too. You cannot just spell out 1-2-3 about arthritis to a six-year-old, and information presented to a teenager is completely different. The needs of different ages are not the same. Ask lots of questions. You won't do this, but test yourself after the sessions to see how much you learned. You'll be surprised by how much you missed; then ask more questions later. Another version of this is the inquisition later at home from your indispensable other. Make him go, too, and save time.

Another thing—just because you've gone through this exercise at the beginning, remember that in a few years your child is in a different developmental age and needs instruction all over again. When a three-year-old becomes a six-year-old, what she or he needs to know is different.

Again, do your dead-level best to persuade your husband or indispensable other to participate and come to the educational sessions. Fathers far too often do not participate for reasons discussed in Chapter 3 on emotional adjustment.

The Nutritionist

The nutritionist will discuss normal nutrition with you. Now don't get your nose out of joint because someone tells you about normal eating habits and diet. The vast majority of Americans can't tell you the names of basic foodstuffs, much less how much of each is needed. There is no special diet for children with JRA, just a proper general diet. An excellent pamphlet, *A Food Guide for the First Five Years*, is listed in Appendix C. It's good—get it and read it. A really great guide for all ages is a front-and-back outline published by the National Dairy Council, *Guide to Good Eating*. It's also in Spanish—see Appendix C. Two other great pamphlets are *Dietary Guidelines for Americans* and *Diet and Nutrition: Facts to Consider.* Both of these pamphlets are also listed in Appendix C. Children with JRA need a proper diet, and children with poor appetites due to the illness or side effects of medicines may need special advice to keep the diet adequate.

Much of the poor weight gain and growth in JRA is due to poor nutrition rather than the disease itself. Nutritional anemia is a common problem, and the nutritionist's help is essential to building iron stores.

Special diets for specific medications are important. Cortisone meds cause retention of fluids in the body and can cause hypertension. The nutritionist team member will instruct you in a low-salt diet to reduce the weight gain. Anticipatory advice is another service by the nutritionist. She will give you information about food fads and bizarre cures for arthritis.

Special Education Counselor

Only one center to my knowledge has a special education counselor on the team. This is the team in Houston. We added him to the team a few years ago to see whether a teacher and counselor from the school system could be a more effective liaison to the schools. There is such a difference in approach and mind-set between teachers and medical people that an interpreter is probably needed. You can feel the change in attitude when a medical pro calls a teacher and when a fellow teacher calls. The fellow teacher gets the services needed a lot faster and a lot more often. The experience has been extremely successful. Teachers warm up more readily to a fellow teacher than to a health professional, and the counselor has been invaluable in helping health professionals and parents to understand the problems of the schools.

Parent-Pal

Pie-in-the-sky stuff, but I want to tell you about it anyway. The idea has surfaced in several places to have an experienced and articulate parent on a team to give support to families and advice from one parent to another. The idea has not caught on, to my knowledge, and is hung up on the usual—how to pay them.

Designated Person

As you and the team become better acquainted, a member of the team will stand out as the one with whom you are most at ease. This person should become the designated person for contact rather than the coordinator. If the team is not familiar with this concept, show them this book. They may like it; if not, we tried.

Tests and More Tests

In addition to the evaluation by the team, there are tests that are necessary to either diagnose the illness, rule out other illnesses, or determine the extent of disease or complication. The laboratory tests (blood and urine needed) are sometimes many in number, and Elizabeth's aversion to those dreaded words, *blood drawing*, is real. In fact, to most children, it's not a big deal. The technicians are usually pretty slick at obtaining blood specimens. The blood tests include a blood count, of course, to see if anemia is present and the other types of cells are OK. The "survey chem" does about 20 or so tests of such things as liver function, blood sugar, and kidney function. The rheumatoid factor test is a blood test along with the ANA. We've already talked about these tests in Chapter 2. The urinalysis is done to find red blood cells, white blood cells, or protein indicating problems with the kidneys.

X-rays are necessary to determine whether some other disease is present, or complications of JRA are already present. X-rays are ordered less now than they were years ago. Sometimes, what is called a joint/bone scan is necessary. This test involves injecting a little radioactive liquid into a vein, and the technician reads a Geiger counter to see if joints are inflamed. The test shows up positive when there is increased blood supply to an inflamed joint. Another more exotic test is magnetic resonance imaging. By using magnetism techniques and changing the direction of the magnetic poles of chemical elements in the cells, technicians can image muscles and joints; the detail is amazing. The procedure is helpful in such special situations as detecting excessive fluid within the hip joint. These findings guide the doctor to earlier treatment with more potent drugs to reduce injury to the joint.

The Team Follow-Up

After the team has looked over the findings and discussed them, a follow-up visit is scheduled for a team conference with the doctor and you. The doctor leads the meeting and explains the diagnosis. A plan is developed with your participation that includes medicines, a physical therapy plan, school services, nutrition, family support plans, other community-based service needs, and psychological services if needed. If eye problems are found, a follow-up is planned.

Here's an important concept of team care: Make sure that your pediatrician or family physician gets a copy of the plan and a phone call from you and the team. Having practiced in a small town for a few years, I am painfully aware that the centers don't keep the primary doc informed. This is important because the first person you'll call after seeing the big center is your primary physician. You must keep in touch with your main pediatrician or family physician because ongoing pediatric care is not provided by the center. This includes immunizations, developmental checkups, and other problems unrelated to arthritis. Even more important, when your child awakens at 2 A.M. with high fever or pain, you need good relations with your primary doc. (I know—they send you to some emergency room now, but at least they call him.) Coordinated care means that your main doctor is part of the plan. This is particularly important if you live in a city or town far away from the center.

Tips About Team Care

Now that we've gone through a trial run, you have to be wondering how this team thing is going to work. Probably the best way to help you to use the team's services properly will be to give some tips and examples of services that the team can provide for you.

In tennis, success is measured by the sequence of hitting the ball over the net, inside the court, and out of reach of your opponent's racket. Coordinated care by the team is the same—a series of appropriate services orchestrated at the right time at the right place. Look at the team as a group of health professionals who are your friends and want to help.

Now let's talk about these community-based services that your child may need. They include the most important one—the school. Other examples are parent support groups, vocational training, psychological and counseling help, transportation, trying to figure out how to pay the bills for a chronic illness, day care, baby-sitting, and home rental of equipment. Let's talk about some examples to show how each works.

School

The work of children is school, and here is where the team is the most helpful. By planning what help or special programs are necessary at school with the team, a united front to the school is possible and success is assured. **School personnel need a defined school liaison program.** What does that mean? It means that you can't blast in there and say, "Oh my goodness, my daughter has JRA. You must help her." Teachers are interested in what deficits and limitations JRA presents and how to modify or change school activities to accommodate your daughter's needs.

For starters, one person should be the contact person; this is best done by the parent (almost always the mother—you). Make an appointment with the teacher. Take pamphlets provided by the team. The best one is *When Your Student Has Arthritis: A Guide For Teachers*, published by the Arthritis Foundation (see Appendix C). Also take along the written instructions by the team for physical education or classroom modifications. You will find the teacher most interested and helpful. She's also overworked, so the more specific you can be, the better results for your daughter. **Always suggest practical written solutions.** For example, state that a pencil holder will be sent to reduce fatigue in writing if arthritis of the fingers is a problem. The child should be allowed to rest her fingers after every 10 minutes of writing, or she should be allowed to move around the classroom every 30 minutes for a minute or two to get rid of inactivity stiffness (Chapter 2). The need for time between classes and allowing your child to do missed schoolwork at home instead of being homebound altogether are other examples of practical solutions that can be written for the teacher.

Last tip for this area: Remember that your daughter gets older every year, and the teachers change. Also, her developmental needs change, so check with the team on this issue at least once a year.

The second tier of school liaison is a specific letter to the teacher or school nurse provided by the team. Medication letters are necessary to permit teachers or nurses to give your daughter medicines during school hours, typically at lunch. Again, you are the direct liaison. Physical education letters that modify physical activities also need to come from the team. I suggest that you take the letters and personally explain the instructions rather than send them in a note with the child.

The third tier is when a member of the team calls or goes to see a teacher, nurse, principal, or physical therapist. In our center the social worker went to difficult Individual Educational Plan meetings. Sometimes individual school personnel need help in understanding a problem. There's nothing like a member of your team showing up at school to help them understand. An example of a team member dealing directly with the school is when a child with JRA requires a cortisone medication and needs to restrict salt in a big way to reduce too much weight gain from fluid retention. The nutritionist will either send a special diet by letter to the food service department or telephone the food service supervisor. On rare occasions, a school will have a case manager to handle these problems. In my experience, the nutritionist calls the cafeteria supervisor and makes a deal.

Family Support Services

Here is where the team will totally pay for itself in service to you. They can put you in touch with another parent or parents who have been down the trail. Just to talk to someone early on in your journey with JRA is worth its weight in gold. The team will also put you in touch with the AJAO and its regional and summer get-togethers with other parents, children, and professionals. The regional meetings need not be expensive, and the AJAO local chapters pay the expenses to send parents from some areas.

Vocational Training

In Chapter 8 we discuss the need to start early with work expectations. Ask the team about the job awareness program that the National Children's Medical Center in Washington, D.C., has innovated. This will be important to your teenager.

If you perceive that your daughter will not go to college, start early with vocational planning. Vocational services are available in many states at even younger ages for planning. The team can open these doors and make the proper phone calls for you.

Psychological and Counseling Services

The social worker on the team is usually very able in helping with situational problems as they arise, such as brothers and sisters who are jealous, angry, or whatever. It is good to remember that the social worker can help when things get strained with your spouse or indispensable other. At times the whole situation can be severe enough that the team will recommend help from psychological services.

Transportation

If you're a one-car or no-car family and have limited financial means, transportation is sometimes a big problem. Taking the bus to umpteen appointments or trying to get on the school bus with kids jostling your daughter is very real if you're faced with it. In many states the team can arrange for the metro or whatever your town calls the bus system to pick up your daughter in a special van, if necessary. It's usually a hassle, but it can be done.

If you live far enough away from school, the school bus can be a never-ending problem in my experience. Use the team in full force with this one. On several occasions I have personally called a principal at school to help her understand how important it is to help. Kids with severe morning stiffness and pain, with limitation of motion of joints, have a heck of a time waiting for the bus on a cold corner with the wind blowing. Special bus service is possible if you're persistent.

Help with Paying the Bills

No, the team can't write a check, but there are several ways the team can help in certain situations. If your income level qualifies, state services may be possible in many states. This can include payment for some of the clinic and hospital bills or equipment at home. The social worker is the wonder person here. The paperwork is usually so complex that a law degree is helpful, but the team can really clear the path better than you can.

The team can go to bat for you with insurance companies who try to get out of paying bills that are covered. Some companies make a science of asking for more information to delay or avoid payment. My colleagues in the USSR, who are part of our USA–USSR scientific cooperation program, mistakenly believe that they fill out more forms than American doctors do. It's a close call. Another common ploy of insurance companies now is to cancel your policy when JRA is diagnosed or becomes too expensive. The team can be helpful here also.

While we are on the subject of costs, as you have already discovered, or soon will, most companies will not pay for home or outpatient physical therapy visits. They sometimes will pay for what they call modalities (sticking a foot in a paraffin bath, whirlpool, or steam cabinet), but they will not pay for education about exercise and visits to check progress with your home program. They will also not pay for team care. In fact the medical director of one of the largest health insurance companies in the United States not only refused to pay for team care but wanted a blind study to show that helping families coordinate physical therapy and other services was useful.

One last place the team can be of service regarding insurance and financial matters is when you try to get life or health insurance after your daughter is too old for your policy. We talk about this in Chapter 8, but the subject is so important that a little repetition won't hurt. The team will be up-to-date on the few companies that will write health or life insurance for your daughter. The price may be out of sight.

Having Fun

The last example of team tips and how to get the most out of your team is to go to the fun things the team arranges. During my last years directing our center, we had an Easter egg hunt every year at our house or a park. I dressed in an Easter bunny suit and sunglasses—the team even videotaped it one year. We also had family retreats and picnics; we had discussion groups, but mostly fun.

Many pediatric rheumatology centers have summer camps for kids with JRA. Be sure to ask the team to keep you informed and to sign your daughter up before they are full. Trying to get into regular camps can be tough because they will not give meds and worry about the liability. See Appendix D for a list of previous camps.

Care Coordinators

For four years (1986 to 1990) I worked full-time with the Maternal and Child Health Bureau as a consultant to help develop what we now call family-centered, community-based, coordinated care for children with special health care needs and their families. We promoted care coordination, team care, and family-to-family network organizations. During this time I found to my sorrow that no system exists to help families of children with special needs to gain access to the needed community-based services already mentioned. Time after time a hurried prescription or verbal plan is given at the hospital or office. There is no system or interest in really accessing these services. In particular, so-called discharge plans for children with complex illnesses were written by hospital staff members with no provision for carrying them out. These activities need to be done by care coordinators—in your situation, call that team care. Busy family physicians or pediatricians who want to be the medical home for families do not feel that they can spend the time necessary to arrange for services needed by the child or family. Even worse, the insurance carriers, if you can believe it, will not pay someone to coordinate complex medical and social services needed to help your child and family do better. They don't mind paying for expensive hi-tech tests or treatments but they will not pay to assure that a coherent plan is actually drawn up and carried out. They certainly have coordinators to process paying those bills or denying them.

The number of services are into the hundreds, and when needed are essential to good care. Yet more times than not, the family is unaware of the help that is in place. Time after time I encountered parents who did not know that they could receive better help with special school services or be eligible for some state financial aid. No one would tell them about support groups or how to find special clothing or equipment.

In my view accessing needed services for children with arthritis and other special needs should be as easy as accessing restaurants in the Yellow Pages.

So aren't you lucky that you have a pediatric rheumatology team to help you access those services? It is very difficult for an individual doctor with no team to help you properly.

End of soap-box section. Thanks for reading it.

Care by an Individual Doctor Rather Than a Team

Well, we certainly had individual doctors long before we had teams. Of course, it's possible. Some adult rheumatologists feel strongly that they are just as qualified or more qualified to care for children with rheumatic disease than pediatric centers are. My suggestion is that if you live in a town with no pediatric rheumatology center, have your pediatrician arrange with an adult rheumatologist to supervise care as needed, but try to have at least an initial evaluation at a pediatric rheumatology center. Them's my sentiments.

5

Keep on Moving: Physical Therapy

From what I have observed in the course of my daughter's illness and also in that of many other children, I firmly believe that physical therapy is one of the most important ways to minimize your child's physical impairment. The various types of exercise and heat treatments are meant to strengthen muscles, stretch contracted muscles, and maintain a full range of motion. While the physicians try to find a way to control the disease, you have the opportunity, or, if you prefer, the obligation, to help maintain your child's mobility. Don't be frightened by the term *physical therapy*. There's nothing mysterious about it. It's simply moving the muscles and joints to keep up normal strength and normal motion.

When an adult is diagnosed with rheumatoid arthritis it is in all probability going to be a lifelong struggle. But many children with arthritis will experience a remission. Some will have a "spontaneous remission" in which the disease will disappear as rapidly as it appeared. They are the fortunate ones. But as long as your child is facing this problem you must do everything you can to help her avoid permanent disablement through physical therapy.

There are several ways to approach the problem. Rather than drive to the medical center two or three times a week, with the frustration of trying to find a parking place, and frequently having to carry Elizabeth, we decided to do our exercises at home. The physical therapist at Texas Children's Hospital prescribed the proper exercises for her specific problems, taught us how to do them, and gave us a booklet with drawings describing them.

This was our decision. Since I was at home with the children it made sense in our lives. I have met many parents who tell me that they could never have done this for their child. You are basically taking a child already in considerable pain and inflicting more pain. I do not minimize the effort. There were days in which I was on the floor helping Elizabeth, and I was in tears, too. I understand the reticence of many parents to pursue this course.

If this is how you feel, then you must find alternate ways to get therapy for your child. Unfortunately, if you feel that you cannot work with your child the next step is to take her to a physical therapist who will help her. Earl and I have had the experience that most insurance companies will not pay for these treatments. Another possibility is to see if your child's school has a therapist who can help. I cannot emphasize enough how very important it is to be diligent in this effort. I fully believe that Elizabeth would be in a wheelchair today without the tremendous effort we all expended. And I assure you that it was worth every second!

Twenty-five years ago these children were either put to bed or placed in full body casts. Either course soon led to total atrophy of the muscles and joints. The only recourse was to wait until they stopped growing and then consider joint replacement. So they were looking at a youth spent in bed and in a wheelchair. Severe deformity. Hands were gnarled, the back was bent, the vigor we associate with youth disappeared. And that is only the physical side of the equation. Imagine your childhood spent confined to bed. You are deprived of the social aspects of developing with your peers, your education surely suffers, your emotional development is altered dramatically.

On a visit to the therapy unit at Children's Hospital in Los Angeles, I met a boy of about 12 years of age named Jesús. He was from a very poor rural area of Mexico and had been brought to the hospital by relatives. No one in his village really understood what was wrong with him. No one there understood that children could have rheumatoid arthritis and he had been misdiagnosed. He had been given herbal tea and other folk remedies. Obviously to no avail. When he arrived in Los Angeles he was curled up in the fetal position, unable to straighten his body. I met Jesús about a month after his arrival and he had a grin from ear to ear. He could not walk yet, but he was able to lay straight on the bed and move his limbs. He was absolutely certain that he would be walking before long. Of course the treatment with medications had helped, but primarily it was because of the extensive physical therapy that he felt so encouraged.

Fortunately, physicians today realize the importance of keeping their patients moving and active. Because of this approach many people have been able to avoid painful and expensive joint replacement surgery. But also, even if joint replacement is necessary (and they are doing wonderful things in surgery today), you need to maintain muscle strength before and after surgery.

With this background knowledge, Elizabeth and I began a rigorous course of physical therapy. We had a family conference and decided that we would all pitch in to help with the program. It was necessary to do the exercises in the morning and the evening. We agreed that Sunday would be a day off—no therapy. I mean, even God rested on the seventh day!

Physical therapy may range from very structured exercises (with the advice of a trained physical therapist) to unstructured exercise such as swimming, or even playing with clay or stretching large rubber bands to strengthen the hands. A good physical therapist will have a multitude of tips to entice your less-than-enthusiastic youngster to participate in the exercises.

In Elizabeth's case we really organized our bathroom into a "physical therapy unit." We had a large whirlpool with a jacuzzi, but even if you don't have a tub that circulates the water, just soaking in a tub will do wonders. A friend in Los Angeles, a young woman who is unable to get in and out of a tub by herself, tells me that what saves her is just taking a very long, very hot shower every morning. Hot water is one of the most blessed reliefs for a person with arthritis. It definitely helps decrease the pain and loosen stiff joints.

When Elizabeth was in so much pain that she could not do the exercises the therapist recommended on "dry land," we retreated to the whirlpool. After about 15 minutes in the hot water she was usually able to do them. Sometimes keeping this 11-year-old in the water was the real challenge! I remember lying on the floor next to the whirlpool creating a puppet show with my hands. We drew funny faces on my hands, and I sang and made up really stupid jokes. Occasionally a line from a Broadway show came to mind: "If my friends could see me now!"

Through trial and error, and based on which joints were swollen and inflamed on any given day, we eventually developed a daily routine. When Elizabeth made the decision that she wanted to continue in her regular classes as long as she could, the morning therapy sessions became extremely important.

Elizabeth's arthritis was so aggressive that within five months of diagnosis we decided to put her bed downstairs in our bedroom. For one thing, she was waking up every two or three hours screaming in pain. For another, she had begun to have "ulnar drift," a condition in which the hands begin to turn outward. In order to stabilize the joints the occupational therapist had fitted her with splints on both arms, fastened with Velcro straps, which had to be worn every night, and occasionally during the day. This pretty much immobilized her hands, and walking was extremely painful, so I decided that it would be easier for all of us to have her nearby at night.

Because Elizabeth was determined to remain in her regular classes, we had to get up at 5:30 A.M. to begin filling the whirlpool with hot water. When it was full I carried her crying with pain to the bath. We put a small TV there to help distract her. I would then prepare her breakfast. I had a man make a lucite tray that fit across the top of the tub. She would have her breakfast in the blessed hot water. She took her morning medication, and by then the stiffness had subsided enough to permit her to do her exercises.

We brought a hydrocollator from her father's office. It is a large metal tank containing hot water and pads of different sizes filled with silicone, and it provides a very effective method to get deep heat to the large joints. We also had a hot paraffin bath. This is a small electric tank containing melted paraffin with wintergreen oil. It is used in beauty salons for manicures, but in this case we used it to heat the small joints of the hands and feet.

After Elizabeth had finished her exercises, I would lift her from the tub and wrap her in a large towel. Then we would dip each hand about 15 times in the melted paraffin, wrap a plastic baggie around the hand, wrap a towel around that, and place rubber bands around it to hold it in place. We repeated the process with each foot.

While she was in the tub, I arranged the hot silicone pads on the bed, depending on which joints were most swollen. On different days either her knees, hips, elbows, or shoulders would need the extra heat, frequently all of them. (At one point she had 46 joints swollen and inflamed.) After we prepared the paraffin, I carried her to the bed, placed her on the prearranged hot pads, covered her, and turned on the morning talk shows. (At 11, this child knew virtually *everything* happening *anywhere* in the world. Her history teacher, bless his innocent heart, commented on how well informed she was. If he only knew why!) I also had an ultrasound machine at home that instilled very deep heat into the large joints.

In the evenings physical therapy became a family event. I would prepare dinner and Elizabeth's father, brother, sister, or sometimes all three, would help her with her exercises. Some of them required help with resistance exercises, but *all* the exercises required encouragement!

During this time Elizabeth could hardly walk. We had the good fortune to have a swimming pool in our yard, and on warm days I would carry Elizabeth to the pool. The water has the incredible effect of alleviating pressure on the joints. It must be like the weightless effect the astronauts feel in space. You can imagine how fatigued I was with the ritual of therapy combined with the sleepless nights. My pleasure was to get into the pool and lay quietly on a float. Elizabeth would wait until I was totally relaxed, then swim under my float and flip me over.

The water is a wonderful freedom for people with arthritis. The local chapters of the Arthritis Foundation have aquatic programs, and I recommend them highly. Check to see if your local YMCA has a swimming program for children. Also, most communities have health clubs with heated pools, and they will usually permit children if you accompany them. Children and water are always a happy mix.

About this time one of Earl's other patients described how much a water bed had helped her restless nights. You guessed it. That day we went out and bought one. The water is heated from below by a large heating pad. You can fill it until you are comfortable with the firmness. There seems to be less pressure on the joints in a water bed, and the warm temperature also helps. The morning after the first night Elizabeth slept on the water bed, I awoke about five o'clock, shook my clock, and checked to make sure she was all right. For the first time in many months she had actually slept all night. Unless you have been deprived of deep sleep over a long period, you will not understand the joy with which I met that morning.

Elizabeth, today, is a very active young lady. When she first saw an adult rheumatologist the doctor could not believe, looking at her medical records, that she was not more severely impaired.

I attribute this wonderful fact to the aggressive way in which we attacked her arthritis, and to the amount of physical therapy we did. I cannot emphasize enough to every parent and child with arthritis the importance of following the prescribed regimen. It is not an easy path! But I cannot imagine seeing my child in a wheelchair and looking back with regret because I did not do everything possible to help her.

Earl Makes a Case for Exercise

Sometimes I am asked the question, "If you could prescribe only one treatment, which one would it be?" **Physical exercise.** Physical therapy is more important than any other thing you will do. The bottom line is preserving and improving muscular and joint function.

To bring home the point, let's say that because of an injury, your arm must be strapped and bandaged to your chest for three weeks with no motion. Then the strap is removed. Guess what happens when you try to move your arm? You can't move it, nor can you move your shoulder. That's very impressive when it happens to you. If an active exercise and motion program is not begun at this moment, normal motion in the shoulder may be permanently lost. The muscles will also need intensive therapy to increase strength and endurance.

How does this relate to your child? We know from a number of studies, and just common sense, that when a knee hurts most of the time or has swelling, there is usually a limp. The child is not using the bad leg as much as the good leg, and even worse, she is overusing the good leg. The muscles of the painful leg weaken quickly, the calf and thigh become smaller, and that leg demonstrates less endurance and earlier fatigue than the good leg. The appearance is unsightly, but even more important, the good leg takes over and your child develops pain in the knee or hip of the good leg from excessive use. Like most things in life, it's easier to keep what you have than recover what you've lost. Once these events have set in, the road to getting muscle endurance, size, and strength back is long and difficult.

So the lesson is to begin physical exercise as soon as pain or swelling begins. It's not smart to wait until trouble sets in because set in it will. Pain alone causes disuse atrophy (loss of muscle mass), so don't wait for trouble. Your physical therapist and rheumatologist are going to be in charge of setting up a specific exercise program for your child. In general, each morning a warm bath is the first event to get those muscles going and reduce stiffness and pain. Before the effect of the heat has a chance to wear off, your child will do general exercises for posture and strength, followed by specific individualized exercises. Later in the day the exercises will be repeated again. Diagrams and instructions can be found in the Arthritis Foundation's *Understanding Juvenile Arthritis* and my (and my colleagues') physical exercise pamphlet, *Patients' and Parents' Physical Therapy Handbook* (see Appendix C).

Orthopedists, in my experience, have always been tuned in to physical therapy and team care. They make valuable allies in trying to help your child, and also can plan a physical therapy program if necessary. In fact the orthopedist is probably the person who will suggest that you see a pediatric rheumatologist for help. The orthopedist will probably be the person to prescribe splints or braces if needed, although physical medicine specialists sometimes do that, as well.

Hopefully your child will never require surgery, but there are truly spectacular results from joint replacement now in older teenagers. These young people who were previously doomed to bed or wheelchair are now happy, working, and active citizens.

In the same way that proper exercise is essential, proper rest of the body is also essential. Even without exercise, JRA produces fatigue all by itself. So does pain. For this reason time must be allotted for rest each day. Sometimes this means lying down in the afternoon. It means making sure that plenty of sleep is programmed at night. If pain is severe enough, sleep is difficult, and relief of pain also allows better rest.

Heat, Cold, and Exercise

We know that heat relaxes the muscles and allows motion to occur more easily. Some forms of heat seem to work better than others. Moist heat is the best and most available—a warm bath. Other forms of heat used just before or during exercise are conveniently divided into moist and dry heat. Moist heat includes—yes—heated swimming pools, hot packs, steam baths and cabinets, hot tubs with circulating warm water, and heated paraffin baths. Dry heat includes saunas, ultrasound, and diathermy (deep heat produced by electric currents). Heated water beds provide both heat and motion to help stiffness and pain. Sleeping bags also provide dry cocoon heat to reduce morning stiffness.

In general a warm bath before an exercise session reduces pain and spasm of muscles, allowing better exercise results. Heat also is helpful in reducing or eliminating morning stiffness. In some situations exercises are done more easily in the water because the buoyancy of the water allows pain-free movement. Elizabeth's mermaid abilities in the pool were a result of this relief of pain.

Hot packs are useful for specific, painful joints and muscles such as the knee. Application for 10 minutes or so before an exercise session really helps, or, instead of using a hot-pack machine, moisten a towel and put it in the microwave for a minute or so: voilà—hot pack. How long and how much heat are issues for you to work out with your doctor or physical therapist.

A word about cold packs. This is going to sound strange to you, but some children say that cold packs help their pain and muscle spasm better than heat. If it works that way, use cold packs. They can be purchased; some people keep them in the deep freeze and defrost to the right coldness.

A steam cabinet or room is another example of moist heat. I personally like steam rooms or showers as an excellent way to achieve relaxation of muscles and relief of pain. Hot tubs with circulating water offer an excellent way to get heat and muscular relaxation. The circulating water massages the muscles to relax.

The paraffin bath is heated paraffin/oil in a deep-fryer type of container with a thermostat. Paraffin melts at about 120° or so and allows more heat to be applied to a foot or hand than a hot bath. The body can stand more heat with a paraffin/oil mixture than it can with plain water.

Saunas provide dry heat and in my experience are not as effective as moist heat in reducing pain, stiffness, or spasm. Besides, saunas are not part of American homes except in unusual situations. Ultrasound treatments are based on the ability of high-frequency sound to heat up deep tissues such as muscles and joints in the body. If ultrasound helps pain and stiffness better than a bath, use it but ask your doctor about it. Usually it's expensive and not available at home. The same rules apply for diathermy, a form of deep electrical heat. Ultrasound and diathermy, though, are rarely used in children because of concern about effects on growing bones.

An amazing discovery for me several years ago was how well water beds provide enough motion and heat to prevent or reduce inactivity stiffness and pain in the morning. Certainly for Elizabeth the water bed was more important than anything else we had tried at that point. It's not only deductible as a medical expense, but a few insurance carriers will pay for it as physical therapy equipment.

Types of Exercise

Several categories of exercise are helpful: active, passive, active assistive and resistive, aerobic, isometric (those health club machines), and underwater.

Active exercise includes formal exercises such as sit-ups, knee bends, touching toes and extending the hips. These are useful in building endurance, when done over a longer exercise period, and strength.

Passive exercise is done by another person moving the muscles through a range of motion such as extending and flexing the knee and hip. These exercises are useful to preserve joint motion when pain is so great that active exercise is not possible.

Active assistive exercise consists of you as a parent providing help in the motion of the exercise. This kind of help is needed when stretching a contracted joint is important.

Active resistive exercise is helpful to increase strength. An example is to have you push against your child's shin while she is trying to extend the leg with the knee bent. The health club machines do the same thing on a more sophisticated level.

Aerobic exercise is designed to increase endurance as opposed to strength. This is low-impact jazzercise, treadmills, rowing machines, bicycles, stair climbing, and even walking.

The best overall exercise, however, is swimming followed by rowing. Underwater exercise is my personal favorite. For instance, Elizabeth could barely walk on dry land due to the pain of weight bearing, but when she was in the water, it was like the weight of the world was lifted. She could swim and dive under the water and move her legs and arms with no pain. She could keep and even gain strength and endurance in her muscles. Even if your child can't swim, walking across a pool in chest-high water is much better for the joints and muscles than walking on dry land when the joints are painful.

Gaining access to a pool on a regular basis can be difficult. The distance is often too great for daily use; more frequently, a pool is not available at all for most of the year. A swimming pool can be partially deducted from income tax if added to your home. If you buy a house with a pool, you're probably out of luck. Some parents deduct one half of the pool cost and all of the maintenance. It's a legitimate expense if you can afford it. One parent built a too-elaborate pool and tried to deduct the whole thing. The IRS challenged it, and at the hearing, the daughter, with a tear in her eye, looked up at the tax judge and asked, "What are three martini business lunches?" They even approved that one. As you know, however, what's allowed by the IRS is variable.

The General Exercise Program

Keep your child active! That means as active as possible. In fact every child needs a general physical exercise program to provide for proper strength and endurance. Arnold Schwarzenegger, as chairman of the President's fitness program, is correct in pleading with all of us parents to provide a physical exercise program for our children.

I am ashamed to share with you that until this year, I did not have a planned physical exercise program for myself. I always thought that all of the walking around I did during the day was enough—this from a doctor who has been promoting physical therapy and exercise for more than 30 years. The amazing discovery for me was how great I felt after spending an hour in the exercise room at the University Club in Houston. The exercise trainer, Roni Schlagel, pretended that

I knew nothing about PT and planned an excellent daily program alternating between endurance exercise and isometric exercise with equipment. I don't know if I'll live longer, but I sure as heck feel great each day.

In the same way that any child needs a planned physical exercise program that includes mainly play, children with chronic illness need such a program even more. Posture training in the standing, sitting, and, yes, lying down in bed position is essential. Adults who slouch in chairs and are humped over when they stand did not come that way. It took years of sloppy posture to mess up their shoulders, necks, and backs.

How do you get such a program? Hopefully you're able to consult with a pediatric rheumatology center team that includes a physical therapist and has the same ideals discussed here. If that's not an option, consult your orthopedist or find a qualified physical therapist or a qualified exercise trainer at a quality health club for a general exercise program for your child. Hey! The adage, "Do as I say, not as I do," won't wash with me. Get in there with your child and feel great, too.

Splints and Braces: To Use or Not to Use?

Almost every mother at some time or other deals with a cast made of plaster or plastic on a leg or an arm of a child with an injury. The purpose of the cast, of course, is to keep the leg still for several weeks or months until the bone heals. With JRA, splints or braces are used to help joints. A splint is like a cast, but it can be easily removed by you. A brace is a device that supports a weak joint and holds the joint still, but has supports made of metal that can be set at different angles of joint motion. It also can be removed by you daily. There are at least four main uses for splints or braces with JRA: recover lost motion; provide active resistance to motion to strengthen joints; brace a joint for better functional stability; and maintain alignment of legs or arms.

There is great controversy and discord among experienced doctors about the value of splints and braces. This includes *when* or *if* to use them. One group feels that continuous splints keep the joint so still that the loss of use and activity produces unacceptable loss of size and strength of surrounding muscles. Some physicians compromise by using splints only at night. Splints and braces are used to solve several different kinds of problems, and you need to understand the basic ground rules.

One controversial issue is whether to use a brace or splint day and night or night only, to allow the child normal functioning during the day. The reason for night use only is to allow motion of the joint during the day to reduce atrophy of muscles and maintain motion. There is also better acceptance by the child. Using splints at night is a pain at best, and many children never sleep properly wearing a brace. One truly has to weigh how upset your child is against the gain. A clear liability of braces in particular is loss of muscle strength and size from the resulting inactivity of that particular joint.

The best use of splints in my opinion is to straighten a contracted or bent joint using what is called a three point splint. A good example is using it to straighten a bent knee. The splint puts pressure on the calf and the back of the thigh; a leather pad with buckles covers the knee cap. Each night, when placed on the knee, the buckles are tightened so that the knee is as straight as possible. It is then removed each morning. The leg is a little straighter each day. It usually works, believe it or not—but not always. Persuading a child and mother to leave it on all night is a trick by itself. The three point splints are usually used for several months at a time.

Another kind of splint provides active resistance, or "dynamic splinting," and in my experience sounds better than it works. To increase strength in the fingers, for example, a splint is devised that uses rubber bands suspended on a metal frame. The rubber bands are placed on the fingers, and the child bends the fingers against the resistance of the rubber bands. This is called resistive exercise. My experience has not been favorable with this type of splint, but the idea is good and it should help with strength and motion of fingers.

Another type of splint is called a resting splint to prevent the wrist from drifting out of place to the right or left. This splint is usually worn at night and is useful to keep the wrist straighter and when a drift of the wrist occurs due to arthritis.

A brace of the leg is used by some doctors to provide better walking skills when a joint becomes unstable. The use is limited in my experience in children with JRA.

School and Exercise

If the arthritis is not severe, you will be faced with your child's desire to keep it a secret at school. If it's not too long ago (as it is for me), remember how you wanted to be just like everyone else and not different. The other side of the dilemma is the need to avoid activities at school that will injure the joints. A difficult thing for teachers to understand is why your child hurts so much in the morning that she may just creep around, but by the end of the day she may be running and playing. As you know by now, JRA is capricious in intensity. The teacher and classmates will need to be convinced of this. Also, your child will need to try hard not to use JRA as an excuse to avoid work or activities.

In this situation the physical therapist (PT) or your doctor can be the most help. The most successful strategy in my experience is for the PT to call the school nurse or physical education teacher to establish rapport. In the absence of either, the homeroom teacher and even the principal are also helpful. If rapport is possible, the PT outlines the program by phone and sends a written program with you to the school. This scheme enables you to have something in writing instead of your word as a parent, and we all know what that means to too many schools.

Go over the program with the teacher and take brochures about JRA with you. The Arthritis Foundation offers pamphlets written for teachers (see Appendix C). Remember that teachers in the present climate of educational disaster in our country are pushed to the wall with ever-mounting chores pressed upon them. Many teachers have far too many students to even teach; to add yet one more thing is sometimes more than they can bear. The more interested you can make the teacher in your child, the better the program will go.

In general, the program for a mildly involved child will be more in the line of avoidance: not running laps if the joints of the legs are involved or not hitting baseballs or tennis balls if the arms are involved. As an example of how this can work, I have known teachers to assign a designated hitter for a girl with arthritis of the hands only and a designated base runner for a boy with arthritis of the legs. More than one severely involved child, who has more joints with arthritis than not, has come to the office grinning from ear to ear to proudly tell me that he is now the team manager. If you get the kids and teacher in the spirit of the thing, your child will have more self-esteem and be more a part of the action. You may even have to become the room mother or a sponsor. This is something you already know, but it applies here, too.

Another bit of persuasion you'll have to achieve with the teacher is related to inactivity stiffness. As you've noticed, your child usually has stiffness after sitting for a while. The stiffness becomes uncomfortable, and your child needs to stand and walk around for a minute or so. The first time this happens unannounced in a classroom, the teacher will be quite upset if she doesn't know what's going on. You and the PT must persuade the teacher to let your child do this if necessary. The teacher worries that discipline will be lost if she makes an exception. If the other kids understand, it works out.

Sometimes planning definite exercises instead of regular physical education (PE) is better. I feel that it should be done at the same time as the class does other physical activities. In what were hopefully the "old days," PE or homeroom teachers banished children to the locker room to clean the floors or showers as a punishment or to make a point with the other students. With younger students, teachers assigned them to clean erasers in the classrooms. Another situation that I regard as unsatisfactory is to assign your child to a study hall and forget about physical exercise. **Don't let this happen.** Children with chronic illness in particular need a planned general exercise program even more than kids with no arthritis. If all else fails, have your child take a study hall and do the exercise program before and after school. If possible, it is more efficient to do one of the exercise sessions at school.

A real problem at school for children who take a while to move from class to class is how to get out of their seats in one class and walk to the next class in five minutes or less. Sometimes you can arrange for them to leave one class after the rush, but then they are late to the next class. More than one child on crutches has been knocked down in the halls or on the stairways in the rush. It's a little like the problem we have in Houston with drivers who routinely whiz through signal lights after they've turned red (and often they're the third car to go through after the red). One way to approach this problem is to try for classes on the same floor. Few schools have elevators, and fewer still can afford to put in an elevator. If you press them too hard, they'll try to homebound your child. Don't let them do it. Also in the old days that still exist in too many schools, administrators organize "special classes" for "crippled children." This poorly conceived idea fortunately has come and gone in most places. If it exists in your school, stay away from it.

In Chapter 7, we'll discuss working with physical therapists employed by the school, but it needs to be said here also. This is the mine field of the century. If you're very lucky, you're in a school district that is not only sympathetic to children with special needs but can afford to do the right thing by your child. The probability that both conditions are present in the same school is close to zero in the United States today. As you know, many states and school districts are facing financial bankruptcy in their educational systems. The first service to go in my experience is physical therapy for children with chronic illnesses. The excuse is that this is medical, and unrelated to school and education. One question to ask the school administration when you are fighting for your child's needs is whether they canceled the whirlpool and physical therapy facilities for the high school varsity football players. Then ask why physically gifted children on the football team receive services denied to physically handicapped children with arthritis. At least you'll make them feel a little guilty.

Final Pep Talk

Remember that the exercise program is essential to preserving muscle strength and endurance as well as normal joint motion. Do the best you can with what you have. The general exercise program is necessary for general body conditioning. The specific exercise program is designed to help specific muscles and joints. Both are equally important. The biggest danger to me is boredom. The exercises become very dull, and your compliance and your child's compliance go way down unless you keep give yourself pep talks regularly.

Another thing that reduces compliance is the nature of the exercise program. Your goal is to preserve what your child already has. It's difficult to believe that it works when all that it does is keep what you already have. The only way to find out its usefulness is to do nothing for a while. Your child will lose strength and size of muscles, and then it's tough to get back to normal.

So trust us. JUST DO IT!

6

Medications and
Medical Problems

Earl will address the subject of medications, since I don't know all the scientific reasons for the effectiveness of all of them. I had to learn the major categories of drugs, why they are given, what are the possible side effects. But I would like to comment to parents about some of the "civilian" kinds of things that you should be aware of.

The doctor will see your child for a very limited time, but you live with your child and are accustomed to how she is likely to respond in any given situation. Some children have more tolerance for pain, for example. All three of my children were different in this respect. Learn to observe your child's reactions unobtrusively, and you must respect your ability to evaluate your child's reactions to various drugs. Don't be shy about asking your child's physician, privately (certainly not in front of your child), what to expect when certain drugs are administered.

There is a tremendous amount of new material to absorb when you begin looking at medications. Many of us have a negative response to anything called "drug." I have friends who don't even like to take aspirin for a headache. But when you are talking about drug treatment for a child with juvenile arthritis you are talking about minimizing the damage to your child's body. These drugs are used, in combination with physical therapy and good nutrition, to keep the disease under control.

It would be good if drugs were not needed, but they are an integral part of the treatment. Taking medications can be a pain in the neck. One of the problems I have heard most frequently is that the child begins to feel better (because of the drug), and the parent or child decides to discontinue them, not realizing the drug is the very reason she is feeling better. The child then has a relapse, and it is even more difficult to bring the inflammation and pain under control. It becomes a real seesaw.

I feel certain that a good physician will try to maintain the minimum dosage to keep your child stable. All these drugs have side effects, and we should all aim to find the balance to keep your child free from symptoms with the minimum amount of medicine. But I cannot overemphasize the importance of taking them exactly as prescribed, observing your child's reactions, and working with the doctor to control the symptoms.

Many of the drugs are "slow acting." Elizabeth had been given gold injections early in the disease because she was having serious erosive damage to her joints. She simply could not tolerate the drug. Her blood chemistries went crazy. When we were running out of other drugs five years later, it was decided to rechallenge Elizabeth on the gold injections. It was six to eight weeks before there was a noticeable improvement in her condition. For years she had been descending the stairs sideways, one very slow step at a time. One morning I was sitting in the dining room, reading the morning paper, when I realized that she was coming down the stairs facing forward, in a reasonably normal fashion. I was very excited, but decided to wait for a few more mornings to see if I was premature in my enthusiasm. That was indeed the first sign that the gold injections had begun to take effect. Seven years later she is still giving herself gold injections. It has been effective in minimizing the erosive damage to her joints. If we had not been patient I'm not sure where we would be today.

As I mentioned, Elizabeth was truly frightened of steroids or cortisone. But several years into her treatment, we were having an extremely difficult time finding the right combination of drugs to control her arthritis. Earl decided it was absolutely necessary to prescribe one milligram a day of prednisone, the prescription name of a cortisone, to try to get the symptoms under control and give her some relief. We all made a concerted effort to explain very carefully to her that this was a minute amount, strictly to help her body regain control.

This was about three years after the initial diagnosis. By this time Earl had gained Elizabeth's confidence, and she was willing to accept his opinion. She was also a lot more knowledgeable in general. I never noticed any adverse effects from the small dosage of prednisone and it did help us get on to the next phase of her treatment.

These are just some of our experiences with medications. It is a tricky path indeed. Don't underestimate how valuable your observations will be. You are part of the "team," so don't be shy in offering your help.

Earl's Pitch

Medicines for children with arthritis help but don't cure. We do our best to get rid of swelling, pain, redness, and tenderness of joints and to improve joint motion. Specific medicines are also used to reduce inflammation in other organs of the body such as the heart, eyes, and kidneys. There's no "penicillin" to cure JRA, but medicines play an important role in the family-centered, community-based, coordinated, comprehensive treatment program.

Great progress has been made in developing anti-inflammatory or anti-arthritis medicines that reduce pain and inflammation. Except for aspirin, most have come to market in the past 20 or 30 years. Many of us feel that we see fewer children with terrible deformities as a result of these medicines. In particular we rarely see the terrible consequences of iritis. It is difficult to say for sure that the better outlook for children is due to medicine alone rather than the whole treatment program. However, the relief of pain and swelling by one or more of these anti-inflammatory drugs allows your child to begin the active, total program. Without significant relief of pain, all physical therapy programs and school service programs are hampered—or worse, not possible—before they even start. I believe that because of aggressive treatment with the newer, available medicines that inflammation is less, and strength, endurance, and joint motion are many times better than in the old days when children were put to bed for months or years.

The immediate goal of drug therapy, therefore, is to relieve pain and swelling as soon as possible. The long-range goal is to alter the progress of the disease itself and its destruction of bone, cartilage, and soft tissues such as muscles, tendons, and joint capsules.

Kinds of Medicines

Two broad groups of drugs are used to treat children with JRA: first line nonsteroidal anti-inflammatory drugs (NSAIDs) and second line drugs. The NSAIDs are always used first because they are usually safer, and if they fail to provide satisfactory relief, second line drugs are added to the NSAIDs. We'll be discussing these drugs later in this chapter.

The NSAIDs frequently used are Naprosyn, Relafen, Ibuprofen (Advil, Nuprin, Motrin, Rufen), and aspirin. The important second line drugs to know about are methotrexate, cortisone (steroids), Azulfidine, hydroxychloroquine, penicillamine, cytotoxic medicines, and gold.

Then there are the unconventional medicines. You may have already received "helpful," well-meaning advice from friends, people on the street, and relatives about arthritis treatments. In any chronic arthritis of unknown cause, where the medicines at best help and don't cure, the number of unconventional remedies are rampant. There are literally thousands of copper bracelets, herbs, medicines, devices, and foods that have helped people feel better (for a little while). The problem is that we know that JRA is a variable disease, and complete or partial relief of pain or swelling of joints may occur for no apparent reason at any time. If a new medicine is taken at the same time that spontaneous improvement occurs, then the new medicine gets credit for the improvement.

At least 8 out of 10 of you will try some unconventional treatment, usually one that's harmless but a waste of time and money. Ask your doctor about the miracle cure that doctors are "keeping off the market" before you rush out and buy it. Each "cure" has a half life of two or three years. The important thing to remember is not to harm your child with a risky fad, or worse, to deny proper treatment for some off-the-wall idea.

General Rules
About Taking Medicine

One reason that so many medicines are available for children with arthritis is that each child responds differently to different medicines. "Different strokes for different folks" is a tenet to remember. A medicine that helps one child may not help another.

Every medicine causes unpleasant or even dangerous side effects in someone at some time. You and your doctor will weigh how much good the medicine can do against how bad its side effects may be in deciding whether to start or continue a medicine. If a medicine helps your child a lot and produces no bad side effects, it's immaterial whether it's dangerous to another child. It is safe for your child, and this is the measure of decision. The prescribed dose is usually started low and increased to a level that either helps to alleviate the arthritis or causes unsatisfactory side effects. You don't need to despair if unpleasant side effects occur. The dose is reduced, and hopefully the side effect will disappear.

The time required for a medicine or an increased dose to effect improvement may be weeks or even months before further change is considered, and follow-ups to check for adverse effects of a drug are necessary. When the physician or nurse asks you to come for a safety check on the medicine, pay attention and do it. It's not just another way to pad the bill. It's important. Often a blood count, urinalysis, and a liver function test are done at intervals of days, weeks, or months depending on the drug and its effect on your child.

Adverse Effects

The usual adverse reactions to drugs are fairly straightforward and can be monitored to ensure safety. Fewer than one child in 20 has to stop a medicine because of bad side effects; aspirin is an exception, with one in six taken off this drug. Anemia, along with a loss of white blood cells or platelets, can occur with almost any arthritis drug. The kidneys also can be injured, as can the liver. A blood count, urinalysis, and liver function are the usual tests done to check on the most frequent side effects of drugs.

Many adverse effects do not require blood or urine to detect. Diarrhea and skin rashes are frequent, for example. Any event that occurs while taking a medicine can be due to the drug but probably is not. If a side effect is not serious, ignore it if the medicine is helping. If it is serious, then you and the doctor will have to weigh how much good the medicine is doing against how much injury the adverse effect is causing. For example, many children get a rash from medicines. If the rash is mild, and the medicine is helping, the heck with it: continue the drug.

Being sure a side effect is due to the medicine is important. The doctor will usually ask you to stop the medicine for a week or longer to see if the rash or blood in the urine disappears. When it disappears, he or she will ask you to restart the drug. Many times, strangely enough, the rash or blood in the urine does not recur; therefore, the rash or blood wasn't due to the medicine. You can thus continue. You see how important it is not only to stop the medicine but to rechallenge the body to be sure a drug side effect has occurred.

When a New Medicine is Added

When the physician and you decide that a new medicine is needed, several common steps take place. The physician or educator explains how the medicine is thought to work, what dose to take, and which side effects to be alert for. Your child will be directed to take a low dose at first. In one to two weeks she will be asked to return for a safety check. Usually a blood count, urinalysis, and perhaps a liver function test will be done. Sometimes other tests are necessary. Also, you and your child will be asked about any side effects such as diarrhea, abdominal pain, headaches, blurred vision, or drowsiness. Most medicines don't take effect so quickly, and improvement isn't expected by this initial checkup. If your child feels better, consider yourself lucky.

The next safety check and office visit will probably be in a month or two, depending on the medicine. In the case of NSAIDs, continuation for at least two and maybe three months is necessary to be reasonably sure that the drug will (or will not) work. In the case of the slower-acting drugs such as methotrexate, a six-month trial is necessary before giving up. *Patience is the hardest lesson to learn, especially when your child is stiff and hurting.*

During my 30 years of caring for children with arthritis, the most frequent reason for a referral from other doctors was that none of the medicines were effective any longer. Nine times out of ten, the many possible medicines had not been given sufficient time to work. Even worse, a subsequent doctor may think that you've tried a long list of medicines and really all that has been done is to run the risk of adverse effects with no chance to see if they work. *Remember! If you badger your doctor to change medicines every few weeks and don't give the medicines a chance to work, you'll never find a medicine that helps your child!*

When the Medicine Quits Working

Of course, medicines do sometimes quit working. There's nothing more distressing than when aspirin, gold, or Tolectin controls the pain and swelling satisfactorily for months or years, and then suddenly quits working. You haven't done something wrong. On rare occasions the druggist has substituted a generic drug of another company which is so different that the helpful effect is gone. Usually, however, the medicine just stops working. We call this tachyphylaxis, and it is not your fault. When tachyphylaxis occurs, your doctor may stop the medicine and start another. Sometimes increasing the dose helps, but then adverse effects can be a problem. Usually another medicine is necessary. In my experience the failed medicine can be started again months or years later and be effective. It's almost as if whatever suddenly blocked the effectiveness—perhaps an antibody or immune response—has disappeared.

Nonsteroidal Anti-Inflammatory Drugs (NSAIDs)

NSAIDs are the initial treatment of choice for JRA. They offer the best and safest help in reducing swelling and pain in joints, and in managing fever. Except for fever relief, they begin to help in terms of weeks and not hours. Sometimes they have to be given for months before improvement is apparent. In general, several NSAIDs will be tried before second line drugs are considered.

Many of the currently used NSAIDs have similar qualities and are grouped together. Indeed, many doctors call them "me too" medications because they are so similar in action. They do not contain any cortisone or its derivatives; hence the term *nonsteroidal.* They suppress inflammation—meaning that they reduce swelling, pain, tenderness, and redness—and improve motion; hence the term *anti-inflammatory.*

Their exact modes of action are not known, but all seem to inhibit parts of a chemical cycle in the body that causes inflammation.

The best known NSAID is aspirin. Other familiar names are Advil, Nuprin, Motrin, Naprosyn, and Tolectin. These are approved by the Food and Drug Administration (FDA) for use in children with JRA. Other NSAIDs—Indocin, Voltaren, Feldene, Clinoril, and Orudis—have been approved only for use by adults, either because they have not been studied specifically in kids with JRA or because studies are still in progress.

Aspirin is the original and oldest NSAID and has been in use since the last century. Its use preceded the FDA by many decades. For this reason aspirin has always been an over-the-counter drug. The other NSAIDs are prescription drugs except ibuprofen (Advil, Nuprin, and others). Acetaminophen (Tylenol and others) is considered a pain killer only.

How NSAIDs are Given

NSAIDs are given by mouth. The most commonly used NSAID until a few years ago was aspirin. Now Naprosyn and the ibuprofens are the first NSAIDs prescribed by most pediatric rheumatologists. A few NSAIDs such as the ibuprofens (Advil, Nuprin) and Naprosyn are available in liquid form.The NSAIDs differ markedly in how often they must be given. Some commonly used NSAIDs such as Naprosyn have long blood-level times of twelve to fourteen hours and can be given only two times daily. Other commonly used NSAIDs such as the various ibuprofens, Tolectin, Relafen, and aspirin have two-to-four hour long blood-level times and must be given three or four times daily. Medicines such as Feldene and Daypro have half-lives of more than one day and can be given daily.

Should NSAIDs be given with meals or between meals? Well, the drug level is higher if taken on an empty stomach, but the stomach pain and nausea are also more frequent. Why is this important to you? While a better drug level will be attained with between-meal dosages, your memory is unfairly tested, and you're more likely to remember to give the medicine at meal times. We also know that you remember to give the medicine better when you only have to give it one or two times daily.

It's important to consider the best time of day to give the medicine. Most NSAIDs provide better results if given in higher doses at bedtime and in lower doses during the day. But with the short-acting medicines, daytime doses are just as necessary.

What does all of this mean? When medications are given two times daily, giving them to your child at breakfast and at bedtime with a little food or milk seems a reasonable schedule. When medication once a day is possible, bedtime may be better. Also, when nausea is a problem, giving the evening dose at bedtime is better because the nausea occurs when your child is asleep. No matter what doctors tell you, most NSAIDs keep fever down for no more than five hours regardless of the half life of the medicine in the blood.

What Type of Relief to Expect with NSAIDs

NSAIDs have three main uses: to reduce swelling and inflammation, to relieve pain, and to reduce fever. NSAIDs improve fever the fastest. Reduction in an hour is frequent. Many times, however, several days or weeks are necessary to control the high fever of JRA. In the joint, relief from pain is usually the first noticeable improvement. Then reduced stiffness occurs, followed by alleviation of swelling and tenderness with improvement of motion. Improvement in the joints can occur in a few days' time, but usually weeks and sometimes months pass before noticeable improvement occurs. In fact, the newer NSAIDs such as ibuprofen and Naprosyn have cut the use of cortisone in children with systemic JRA and high fever.

Until a few years ago, aspirin was the universal drug of choice to use in children with JRA. Then Reye syndrome, a disease causing death from liver and brain damage, was shown to be associated with the use of aspirin for children with flu. Use immediately decreased in most places in the United States. The other NSAIDs such as Advil, Motrin, Tolectin, or Naprosyn became the most used. This continues to be true. It is interesting that Reye syndrome virtually disappeared, not only in the United States where aspirin use was sharply reduced, but also in countries where aspirin use was continued.

In addition to aspirin there are at least 10 NSAIDs on the market now. Perhaps 20 or more are in the process of approval by the FDA. Part of the reason, of course, is the competitive spirit of our free economy. Another reason is that not everyone responds to a particular NSAID; therefore, several different ones are necessary. Some NSAIDs represent attempts to reduce side effects such as headaches, drowsiness, or stomach pain and ulcers. Other NSAIDs can be given fewer times daily to increase compliance as mentioned.

When all things are considered, the treatment effects are the same with all of the NSAIDs. No single one is clearly better than another. No single one has side effects that are absent in the others. The difference is that each person responds differently to each drug, and what helps one child will not help another. In addition, if one drug quits working, we need to try another.

What's also important is that every physician has a favorite NSAID that seems to work best for him or her. Also, by using only a few NSAIDs the doctor is more familiar with the dosage variations and usual side effects; this frequently results in better treatment than if he or she uses many NSAIDs on an infrequent basis and is not as familiar with individual variations of each one.

Very few NSAIDs are approved for use in children because separate drug studies are required for children. The approval process is complex and expensive, but a new program has been established by Congress called the Office of Orphan Product Development to help with this problem. There are so few children with arthritis in relation to adults with arthritis that drug companies don't fund many studies on children. Help is on the way, however. Our Pediatric Rheumatology Collaborative Group was established in 1973 to improve this situation and has completed about 20 studies to date, with more in progress.

Don't be surprised if your physician prescribes an NSAID that's approved for use by adults but not by children. In my experience over half of the approved drugs for adults are not approved specifically for children. Pediatricians must use them in special circumstances. This sounds scarier than it is because, so far, no antirheumatic drug that is safe in adults has been found to be unsafe in children.

In general NSAIDs should be given for two months before changing to another NSAID. There is a 50 percent chance that the first NSAID will be effective, as well as a 50 percent chance for subsequent trials of different NSAIDs. It usually takes a trial of two or three NSAIDs before a safe and effective one is found. Usually a second line drug is considered when two or three NSAIDs have been unsuccessful. If destructive arthritis appears or the disease worsens appreciably, second line drugs are usually added. Methotrexate is the most used second line drug that is often times introduced soon after the onset of disease in patients who have significant disability in concert with polyarticular or systemic onset disease.

Possible Side Effects of NSAIDs

While aspirin's side effects are different enough to warrant a separate discussion, the other NSAIDs can be discussed as a group. The list of adverse effects is long, but the major problems are few. The intestinal tract heads the list with nausea, abdominal pain, vomiting, and diarrhea. Anemia and blood or protein in the urine are next in frequency. Headache or drowsiness are infrequent. Changes in liver function are frequent in children using aspirin but not in children using the other NSAIDs.

About 5 percent of children receiving NSAIDs other than aspirin will have to discontinue them because of unacceptable side effects, particularly anemia. Fifteen percent of children receiving aspirin will have side effects requiring discontinuation, most often due to liver function problems, with abdominal pain a close second.

The liver function tests used most often, called transaminase tests, monitor the enzymes the liver uses to break down many chemicals in the body. The tests go by many names, but two are the SGOT or AST and the SGPT or ALT. They must be done weekly at first and monthly later on to be sure that a particular medication is not injuring the liver.

Each liver function test has an upper limit of normal. Many children on aspirin in particular will have slight elevations beyond normal. When the tests are greater than two or three times normal, the doctor will usually tell you to stop the medicine. Later, he may try to lower the daily dose to see if it will still ease the arthritis and not cause the liver function to be abnormal. Again, it's always a battle to find a medicine that alleviates the arthritis enough, yet has minor side effects.

Aspirin produces changes in the liver function severe enough to stop the medicine in about 10 percent of children. This same change occurs only rarely in the other NSAIDs (2 percent or so).

In the same way that aspirin is the usual culprit in producing liver function test abnormalities, the other NSAIDs cause anemia in 2 or 3 percent of children, while aspirin rarely if ever causes anemia unless secondary to an ulcer in the intestinal tract. It's difficult to know sometimes whether anemia is due to JRA or the medicine. Again, the usual sequence for a doctor to follow is to stop the medicine for a week or two (or longer) to see whether the blood count increases. The anemia can last for months or longer. The reason for the prolonged anemia is that the medication has depressed the blood-forming organs—the bone marrow. You should pay attention to requests for a blood-count safety check.

The urinalysis is used to check for blood or protein. When either is present in significant amounts in the urine specimen, it usually means that injury to the kidney has occurred. Aspirin rarely causes this type of problem, which more often occurs with one of the other NSAIDs. The same rules of stopping the drug mentioned before hold here also.

Second-Line Drugs

When NSAIDs alone do not ease inflammation and pain sufficiently, other antirheumatic drugs are added to the program. Cortisone is a second-line drug, rapid in action, and in its own class. Unlike most NSAIDs, several of the second-line drugs take months to take effect and so are termed *slower-acting antirheumatic drugs*. Included in this group are gold, d-penicillamine, and hydroxychloroquine. Gold is the most effective drug of this group and works best in the injectable form. All of them are probably anti-inflammatory in some manner. Methotrexate is a rapid-acting, effective, second-line drug used in children with moderate to severe JRA.

Cortisone (Steroids)

The drug that gets the best results is also the most dangerous. I mean the C word—cortisone. Cortisone, or its better-known derivative, prednisone, came on the scene in the 1950s. Corticosteroids suppress the immune system to reduce inflammation. Initial doses are truly like a miracle. Within days the child loses pain and stiffness, and can run and jump and play. That's pretty heady stuff if your child has been lying in bed crying in pain. The trouble is that the initial dosage will soon need to be increased to maintain the effect. Like hard drugs, it takes more and more cortisone to satisfy. Finally, not only do bad things happen to the body, but the good effect disappears. Even worse, when the dose is reduced, the pain, swelling, and fever come back with a vengeance. In children the worst injury cortisone does to the body is to stop or slow normal growth. This can produce a dwarfed child. By the way, don't confuse corticosteroids with the male hormone "steroids" mentioned in the press in connection with athletes who take them to increase their strength. The two are completely different in that those "steroids" are the male hormone, not cortisone.

We try to use cortisone as a last resort or in severe situations because of its serious adverse effects on the growing child. It is clearly the most effective anti-inflammatory medicine, but the side effects make us think carefully before using. When necessary, however, it is the best and most effective medicine in our cabinet of drugs.

How Corticosteroids are Given

Steroids are given by mouth or injected into the muscle or the veins if necessary. Tablets and liquids are used in most situations. Injections are usually reserved for hospital care. Prednisone is the main steroid used in the United States. Steroid eye drops are the usual treatment of choice for iritis.

What Type of Relief to Expect with Cortisone

When a child is really sick with JRA and slipping fast, nothing controls the disease better than steroids, which quickly control high fever and severe pain and swelling in the joints, and inflammation in the eyes and around the heart. Steroids provide a general sense of well-being or euphoria that helps in relieving pain enough to get your child moving again.

The good news is that your child is running, jumping, and laughing again. The bad news is that when you stop the steroid the terrible pain and swelling may return more powerfully than before. Also, more and more steroid is required to maintain pain relief. Finally it quits working, and the awesome side effects about to be discussed occur. There you are—you can't stop it. With an enormous amount of effort, the dose can be slowly reduced over months and months a little bit at a time until it is low enough to be safe. When tolerated by the body with no serious side effects, steroids can be given in small doses for years with success.

Possible Side Effects of Steroids

It's important to say at the outset that when steroids are given for only a month or two, the serious side effects discussed below do not usually occur. Even in children who require large doses to control incapacitating JRA for months, or years, the side effects will largely disappear after the medicine is stopped, except for reduced or delayed growth. So if steroids don't affect your child adversely, it's the most useful medicine we have.

Increased appetite and excessive weight gain are annoying possible side effects. Excessive weight gain due to increased appetite can be minimized with early and ongoing intervention from a nutritionist in a motivated patient and family. Having said that, it's still a tough problem to handle.

Steroids retard growth in growing children. The dose required to inhibit growth varies with each child. In some children, large doses for weeks, months, or even years do not affect growth. In a few children growth is completely stopped with only a milligram or two daily. This same perplexing effect is seen with the other side effects. When the medication is stopped, growth resumes in a few months, not weeks, if the bones are still capable of growth. If given over two or three years, dwarfism is a serious concern. Having said that, however, many if not most children on low-dose steroids do not sustain serious growth failure. In children who have no apparent loss of the growth curve there is no worry. This may seem too obvious to state, but if a potentially serious side effect does not affect your child, who cares?

Fluid retention, or edema, is another side effect. Children can blow up like blimps and gain 10 to 20 pounds. Such a weight gain is not only unattractive but dangerous because excessive fluid in the body causes hypertension or high blood pressure. When the steroids are reduced or stopped, the high blood pressure goes away.

Steroids also cause a loss of calcium from the bones, or osteoporosis, which can lead to fractures of the back or other bones. Periodic X rays reveal when osteoporosis is excessive. It can also be measured by a densitometer, an electronic device to measure density of bone. Usually the severity of disease must be weighed against the loss of calcium.

"Masking" of infections can be a problem. This occurs when steroids make your child feel better with bronchitis or some other infection, when normally she ought to feel terrible. You are deceived and think that the illness is not a big deal, when it is. Even though this is a definite problem, in my experience this has rarely caused confusion when your child is ill. If in doubt, check with your doctor.

Some children have emotional changes with steroids. Indeed, a good side effect is a euphoria that occurs at times. Unfortunately, behavior problems can also occur. All are reversed when the steroids are stopped.

Methotrexate

Methotrexate alters special chemical processes in the body that affect immune cells and also is anti-inflammatory in action. It has been used in cancer treatment for many years. In the high doses required in cancer treatment, side effects are many. In JRA very low doses are used, thereby reducing side effects. Like virtually all of the medicines we use, methotrexate's exact action is unknown.

How Methotrexate is Given

Methotrexate is usually given weekly by mouth in low doses. It can also be injected under the skin or into the muscles or veins. It is important that laboratory tests of blood and urine be done every few weeks to check for side effects.

A small daily, oral dose of folic acid is often given to reduce or minimize such side effects as oral ulcers, gastrointestinal discomfort, or liver enzyme elevations.

What Type of Relief to Expect with Methotrexate

Methotrexate is in a class by itself in the treatment of JRA. In our recently completed USA-USSR cooperative study, 120 children with severe JRA from both countries received methotrexate once a week for six months. Over 70 percent improved greatly, while out of the group that took an NSAID alone, only 40 percent improved. This is far better than any of the other drugs studied thus far. In some situations the improvement was startling.

Methotrexate is particularly useful because it allows steroids to be given in smaller doses, which reduces side effects. Many times it allows the steroid to be stopped completely.

Methotrexate slows down the rate of x-ray damage in patients with JRA who already have x-ray damage when compared to similar children with JRA who receive NSAIDs alone. Some patients with severe JRA require higher doses of methotrexate to obtain better control of their disease.

Possible Side Effects of Methotrexate

Unlike cortisone, methotrexate does not affect growth. The side effects are the same as those already mentioned with other antirheumatic drugs. In the doses used, side effects have been minimal in study patients. The results were the same with children in both the USA and the USSR.

However, we all worry about future side effects of any drug given during childhood, and methotrexate is no exception. Potential side effects include reduction of sperm cells in boys. If taken during pregnancy, the baby can be affected. It also can cause injury to the liver and lungs; however, the probability is that this drug rarely causes serious problems.

Sulfasalazine (Azulfidine)

Azulfidine is an anti-inflammatory agent containing a sulfa compound and a salicylate. The action as with other antirheumatic agents is largely unknown. It is increasingly being used with NSAIDs and methotrexate.

How Azulfidine is Given

Azulfidine is given by mouth two to four doses daily. As with most other agents, a glass of milk or food reduces abdominal discomfort or pain. This medication can produce hypersensitivity to sunlight and the usual intestinal complaints, headaches, or skin rashes of the other antirheumatic drugs.

What Type of Relief to Expect with Azulfidine

Azulfidine is prescribed more in the past several years and now surpasses such old favorites as gold in frequency of use. It is well tolerated by children and provided significant reduction of inflammation in several studies.

Possible Side Effects of Azulfidine

The possible side effects are the usual: Intestinal complaints such as abdominal pain or upset, diarrhea, or loss of appetite are possible undesirable side effects. Hypersensitivity to light, dizziness, headache, loss of appetite, and skin rash. Rarely sensitivity to sulfa causes problems within the kidney.

Hydroxychloroquine (Plaquenil)

This interesting drug, long a treatment for malaria, also is thought to affect the body's immune system in helping arthritis. It was discovered as a treatment for arthritis when people taking it for malaria noticed improvement in their arthritis. In the USSR and in a few centers in our country, Plaquenil is given to every child with JRA from the first day of diagnosis. It is thought to relieve pain better and reduce the number of flare-ups with bad weather or illness.

In general, I have used Plaquenil as a last-resort medicine when the others failed, and always with other drugs. When it helped, it really helped a lot. So it's worth trying as a far-down-the-list second line drug. Remember: I'm offering opinions. Your physician may think otherwise.

How Plaquenil is Given

Plaquenil is given by mouth daily, or every other day if the size of the pill is too much for the weight of the child. Months and months of treatment are necessary to show effect.

What Type of Relief to Expect with Plaquenil

Plaquenil does seem to relieve pain in many children with JRA. Proponents of its use believe that flare-ups are less frequent when it is used in conjunction with another medication. Like methotrexate it can reduce the steroid dosage necessary in what is called a "steroid sparing effect."

Possible Side Effects of Plaquenil

The side effects are the usual ones: low blood count, blood or protein in the urine, or abnormal liver function. In doses that are high, injury to the back of the eye (retina) can occur. This actually is not a worry in my experience if the dose is low. Children on Plaquenil usually see the eye doctor every 6 to 12 months.

Penicillamine

Penicillamine appears to act on the immune system in unknown ways to suppress arthritis. The drug was found to be helpful in adult rheumatoid arthritis patients by accident. It is a chelating agent that binds heavy metals like gold and removes them from the body in patients with overdosage of gold. Penicillamine, while being used in treatment of gold overdosage in adult patients with rheumatoid arthritis, was noted to reduce the effects of the arthritis.

This is a bottom-of-the-barrel medication to me. Having said that, I have cared for several children who responded only to penicillamine and nothing else. It's always used with an NSAID and even other drugs such as steroids.

How Penicillamine is Given

Penicillamine is given in tablet form daily. It must be given for several months before any effects are apparent.

What Type of Relief to Expect with Penicillamine

Our study group studied d-penicillamine in a controlled study against NSAID alone and hydroxychloroquine (Plaquenil). None of the three was better than the other. As is the case with Plaquenil, penicillamine can reduce the steroid dosage necessary. Selected children improve on penicillamine when an NSAID alone does not help. For this reason, it remains one of the second line drugs used when NSAIDs fail.

Possible Side Effects of Penicillamine

Side effects, while potentially serious, are infrequent. Milder side effects include loss of taste while taking the medicine and the usual effects already discussed in the blood, urine, and liver function tests. On rare occasions a muscular condition called myasthenia gravis can occur.

Gold

Gold has been used in medicine for centuries. Gold therapy has been a mainstay in the treatment of rheumatoid arthritis since the 1920s. The drug acts to suppress inflammation of the joints in ways that are not clear in spite of many years' experience and usage. Until methotrexate was found to be so effective in children with JRA, gold was the most frequently used second line drug in the United States and other parts of the world. Methotrexate is now the most frequently used second line medicine for arthritis, and gold is used infrequently.

How Gold is Given

Gold can be given orally or by injection. The usual way is to give gold by injection into the muscle each week for four or five months. Maintenance injections are then given every two to four weeks indefinitely. Oral gold (Ridaura) may be given daily for an indefinite period of time.

What Type of Relief to Expect with Gold

With gold the first thing that eases is morning stiffness, usually at two to four months. At four to six months, joint swelling, pain, and tenderness begin to disappear. Gold does not reduce the fever of systemic JRA. If you are unable to tell whether your child is better after six months of gold therapy, you and your doctor need to think about stopping the drug and trying something else.

Injectable gold is more effective than oral gold. Oral gold, however, is easier to take and has fewer side effects. When the oral gold is effective, it is preferable to injectable gold. Some doctors begin with oral gold for this reason. If in six months no improvement is apparent, injectable gold is given for six months. The response rate is about the same as NSAIDs—50 percent. Remember that gold is added to the NSAID, not taken instead of the NSAID.

Possible Side Effects of Gold

About 10 percent of children on gold will need to stop because of unacceptable side effects such as anemia, low white blood cell count, or liver function test abnormalities. The kidneys can be affected also. A drug rash can occur but almost always is mild and disappears when dosage is reduced. Only rarely do serious adverse effects occur. The changes are usually reversible if the medicine is stopped quickly. It is most important to follow up with any lab safety checks your doctor requests.

Other Drugs

Several available medicines haven't been studied in children in the United States or haven't achieved popularity. Sulfasalazine (Azulfidine) is an anti-inflammatory drug used in Europe mainly for the relief of pain. Observations by doctors and a few studies are mixed in how helpful it is. In general Azulfidine is prescribed when the previously mentioned drugs are unsuccessful.

Cytotoxic drugs are cancer drugs that can and do cause malignancy themselves. They also cause sterility and birth defects. These drugs are immunosuppressive, meaning that they lessen the body's defenses to infection. They also are more likely to cause serious injury to the blood and such organs as the kidneys and liver. These drugs include Immuran or azathioprine, cyclophosphomide or Cytoxan, chlorambucil or Leukeran. These drugs are used only when all else has failed, and the child is deteriorating so much that there is fear for life or sight.

Future Drugs

Experimental medicines are the hope of the future. Currently, genetically produced antibodies or proteins that block cells or receptors on the surface of cells that do harm to the body are receiving intense interest. If these cells are successfully blocked in their actions, inflammation will be suppressed, and the child's arthritis will be alleviated. Another similar avenue of drug research is the use of intravenous gamma globulin in different types of JRA. The use of special protein antibodies to inhibit or destroy "helper cells" in the body's immune system is another experimental approach in the early stages. Blocking of these cells will also reduce inflammation and improve the child with arthritis.

For now, however, NSAIDs, second line drugs, methotrexate or gold, and the other drugs mentioned in this chapter effectively improve motion and reduce pain, swelling, and inflammation. They allow your child to do physical therapy and begin the road to improvement. Regard them as your friends.

7

"It's a Mine Field Out There!": The School Scene

School plays a major role in the life of a child, second only to her interaction within the family. Even though a child has a chronic illness, it is imperative to maintain her in a regular school setting. Rarely is homebound instruction necessary, except for short periods of time. The social skills children learn by associating with their peers are necessary for future survival and success in the workplace, and of course for a normal life.

At a conference held in Houston to address some of the problems of the chronically ill child in the school setting, I had the privilege to meet Kevin, a most extraordinary young man with cystic fibrosis. He participated in a panel with his mother, another mother and her child with arthritis, my daughter, and myself. Even though he knew that his life expectancy was limited by the cystic fibrosis, he needed to explain to the educators, doctors, and legislators attending the conference the importance of being part of the school experience with his friends. He had just spent more than 100 days of the past year in the hospital, but whenever possible he was at school. He explained that school was part of his dream, the only thing that kept him going, the adventure of life. If they deprived him of the ability to participate in that dream, he had no reason to live.

As I listened to Kevin I began to understand what my daughter had been going through, why she was so determined in her effort to attend regular classes. There was a time when Elizabeth could almost not open doors or carry her books, was terribly fatigued, and was frightened that if someone knocked her down, she would be unable to get up by herself. However, she remained determined to continue attending her regular classes. She had the good fortune to attend a small, private school where everyone was aware of her condition, offered help, and exceptions were made to accommodate her whenever possible, and it was just physically easier to get around. I have also heard accounts from other parents of the same caring treatment in larger public schools. If there was a class upstairs, perhaps a lab class that could not be moved, arrangements were made for the child to take that class in the afternoon when her stiffness had usually subsided enough for her to climb the stairs.

To continue attending her regular classes required an inordinate amount of courage, energy, and determination. She could have opted to stay home with a tutor, which at one point Earl recommended. Our lives would have been considerably easier. But it was so important to *her* to continue that we all decided to do the best we could, as long as we could.

This decision made it necessary for me to be "on call" for her. There were days when she would get to school and simply be too exhausted to continue. Sometimes I had to pick her up; other times the school secretary would let her take a brief nap, after which she was able to continue. If you are a working mother you'll probably have to make arrangements with the school to accommodate your child's need to pace herself. Hopefully you will find understanding people.

I wish I could say that all the experiences I have heard recounted around the country were as happy. One mother told of her six-year-old beginning first grade. Her little hands were so damaged by arthritis that she could not grasp a regular pencil. The mother bought soft rubber pads to wrap around her pencils so she could write. As soon as the teacher saw them she took them away from the child, her reason being that she could not have "anything different in *her* classroom."

Another story came from a 17-year-old who needed to take a French course in order to graduate from high school. The classroom was on the second floor of her school, and her knees were too damaged to climb stairs. When the teacher was asked to move her class to the first floor, her reply was that she had taught the same class in the same room for 17 years and she was not about to move now. You have recourse!

My experiences tell me that the variety of responses from the educational systems around the country vary from: "Please tell us how we can help your child!" to "If your child is *sick* he or she does not belong in class with *normal* children!" For this reason the Federal Government has enacted laws to protect the rights of all children with health impairments. Public Law 94-142 guarantees the right of all children to equal education regardless of physical disabilities. Under this law your child has the right to be evaluated for special services provided by this law. Every eligible child should have an Individualized Education Plan (IEP), developed in collaboration with the parents, school staff, and any concerned specialists.

You will have to evaluate your own situation and determine if it is possible to arrive at an informal agreement with your child's school administration to accommodate your child's needs. If you take this approach, remember that your agreements will not be formally documented and will be difficult to enforce. If you decide to request a formal IEP, you will need guidance through this maze. The American Juvenile Arthritis Organization of the Arthritis Foundation, with funds from the Ronald McDonald Children's Charities, has produced a wonderful manual to educate parents and students regarding their rights in the schools. The title is *Educational Rights for Children with Arthritis: A Manual for Parents*. (See Appendix C.) It is a very comprehensive manual, outlining the whole spectrum of possibilities you might expect to meet as your child moves through the educational system.

The manual explains the laws relating to education and takes you step by step through the formal special education process. You will learn how an IEP is developed and when your child may need home or hospital instruction. There is a chapter on "Transition and Life Planning," and one on what I consider the most important subject— becoming an advocate for your child. It makes me sad to realize that such a basic need, such an important part of any child's life has to be legislated. The reality is that we must protect our children.

I would like to tell you a tale of one school district, which will remain nameless. Earl Brewer's social worker called me one day several years ago, at her wit's end from trying to convince the district's administrators to help an 11-year-old girl with severe polyarticular juvenile rheumatoid arthritis. The child's parents were Hispanic, and the mother did not speak English. Almost every joint in this child's body was swollen and inflamed, and she had been in and out of the hospital. The school officials refused any physical therapy or any special considerations for her. Her wrists were locked in a fixed position, slanting backward and sideways. The officials insisted that, among other things, she could play volleyball. The administrators had become extremely hostile and adamant. An IEP had been requested from the teacher, and the principal and the social worker anticipated a very contentious session. The social worker wanted me to attend, as a parent of a child with arthritis, and because I could speak Spanish. Also, I was acquainted with the system, and am reasonably fearless. When we arrived we met not only with the teacher and principal, but the administrator (a Ph.D.), the assistant administrator, a secretary, and the physical education teacher (three men and three women). On our side we had the mother, who was so frightened she never spoke a word, the social worker, and myself.

Federal law says that you are permitted to tape record the sessions. When we told them that we were going to do so they left the room for a conference. When they returned 15 minutes later, they very unceremoniously unplugged our tape recorder, giving us some very flimsy excuse for doing so.

The social worker began by explaining the disease process. She told them that the physicians were trying to control the disease with medication, but it might be a long process. In the meantime it was imperative that the child receive physical therapy in order to keep her out of a wheelchair. The girl was in considerable pain and should not be required to participate in regular PE classes that would further damage her joints, and so on.

One of the participants on the other side kept interjecting the thought that the child was not in a wheelchair and therefore did not qualify for "services." "And besides, we don't *do* physical therapy!" I knew for a fact that football was very nearly a religion in that district. I asked if they gave their athletes whirlpools and rub-downs after games and taped their sprained joints? "Of course we do!" he replied with astonishment. "Then you do indeed *do physical therapy*," I responded.

We had debated this topic for about an hour and a half when one of the Neanderthals across the table had a brilliant idea. He said, "Well, the way you describe the disease it won't be long until she *is* in a wheelchair. *Then* she will qualify for services!" This man actually thought that he had found the ultimate solution. When we looked at his expression we knew we were engaged in a futile conversation.

Unfortunately, this tale does not have a happy ending. The mother was extremely intimidated by the school administrators and was unable to get them to follow up on the very few concessions they made. Among them, they agreed to let the child use an indoor swimming pool after 9 P.M. Just imagine getting an 11-year-old child with arthritis to a pool at that hour. This is to illustrate how important it is to know your rights and how to go about protecting them.

A year or two later, I was describing this confrontation to the man who oversees the enforcement of Public Law 94-142 from Washington, D.C., for the Department of Education. He told me that he had more complaints about this "nameless" school district than any other in the nation. To which I replied, "But their football team has a terrific record!" My contention is that a child suffering from a chronic illness surely has the same rights as an athlete in the same school. Many school districts may not have facilities to care for the needs of impaired children. But if they have whirlpools, swimming pools, and other equipment for their athletes, by all that is right in this universe, they should be available to any child who needs them. And many of the things that help our children don't require financial support. They simply require understanding, sensitivity, and a desire to help.

Another administrator in a different school district conducted a tour of several of his schools for the state's legislators. At the conclusion of the tour he stated that anyone could see that a child with a disability had no business in his district. This is an obvious violation of Section 504 of the Rehabilitation Act, Public Law 93-112. This Act states that people with disabilities may not be discriminated against because of their disabilities. It includes the right to vote, education, employment, accessibility, and so on. It deals with basic civil rights. As you can see, in order to ensure your child's rights, it is imperative for you to understand the legal rights of your children.

There are many caring educators who understand that they are trained to "educate" your child, whether they are healthy or health-impaired. Unfortunately, there are also many "uneducated" educators who will impact the lives of your children. If you have a young child with arthritis, I cannot urge you enough to write to the Arthritis Foundation, 1314 Spring Street, N.W., Atlanta, GA 30309 (if you call 404-872-7100, ask for the AJAO Department) and request the manual *Educational Rights for Children with Arthritis*. You will find it an invaluable tool to guide your efforts to get the best possible education for your child.

Many of the problems that need to be addressed in the school systems do indeed require a large dose of good will, but many others are a fact of fiscal problems. I made reference at the beginning of this chapter to an educational conference held in Houston. One of the speakers at the conference paraphrased the famous Martin Luther King "I have a dream" speech. She said that her dream would be that one day we would have billions of dollars to take care of all the education and health needs of all the children in the country. And the Pentagon would have to hold a bake sale to raise money to buy another aircraft carrier. Sounds terrific to me!

Earl's Battle Plan

You've heard of Action Jackson? Well, this is the Action Jackson chapter. School is your child's work, and this chapter is geared to show you what she needs to pursue that work. The secret is to plan carefully, and then do what you plan.

Bring together your daughter, spouse or indispensable other, and siblings to review the situation and put together a short-range and a long-range school plan for your child with JRA. You should begin by talking through your fantasies for your child's future. If you don't dream or try for an expanded horizon, you'll never get it. An East Texas special education teacher's imaginary friend, Mr. Williams, philosopher and janitor, said it best:

"If you do what you always done,

You'll always git,

What you already got."

Next, realistically look at the downside of your child's future—the worst-case scenario. Get help here from the team. Find out what might happen with a serious physical disability, and how it might affect what she can and cannot do, for example.

From here the only place to go is up, but seriously, you need to make contingency plans even though you may never need them.

This part is the difference between success and failure. Follow up with three areas of separate discussions. Mom, as usual you're elected to take minutes and notes. Review where your family was before JRA, then review what your situation is now with JRA added to your family. Now, the kicker: plan where you want to go, and then do it!

The plan for the future includes the short-range plan to communicate with all school personnel to provide the best educational atmosphere possible. Friends of your child will need to be brought into the circle of understanding and will need to continue including your child in their activities. Brothers and sisters and, yes, Dad, will need to buy into being active participants in the program. The long-range plan will be ongoing and changing, but you do need to address what options are available if necessary. No one is going to do it for you, but the team can help. In Chapter 8, we'll say more about this.

Sounds a little pie-in-the-sky, doesn't it? To most people it is, but you and I know that it works. You can even get some help with this if you want it. Dr. Suzy Frumess, Assistant Superintendent of Special Education of the Houston Independent School District, gave me a wonderful monograph, *Action for Inclusion: How to Improve Schools By Welcoming Children with Special Needs into Regular Classrooms*. It was written by several authors who are not only teachers but people with special health needs. Order from the Centre for Integrated Education & Community, 24 Thome Crescent, Toronto, Ontario, Canada M6H 2S5. More than likely you'll do just fine with what we've discussed. After all, it's your family and you've been planning things for years anyway. This is just something new.

Communication with School Personnel

The secret to success for a positive school program for your child is proper communication with school personnel. Go back and review the school liaison we talked about in Chapter 4 on team care. Remember that you are the liaison with the school and with your child's teacher. Also remember that you will take along specific written instructions from the team and you. There is specific help for you with this. The following checklist of 39 potential problems for students with JRA was developed by Andrea Kovalesky, formerly of the Children's Hospital in Los Angeles with the staff at her center. It is found in *Understanding Juvenile Rheumatoid Arthritis* by the Arthritis Foundation (see Appendix C.) Use this list to figure out special needs you and your daughter have to present to either the classroom teacher or physical education teacher.

Checklist for Students with JRA

The following is a list of problems that some students with JRA have at school. Remember, every student has different problems, and in order to help your child, it's best to pinpoint those specific to them. So photocopy this checklist, and check off those problems that apply to you. Then review it with your doctor or any of the teachers to whom it applys.

_____ 1. Getting to school is difficult for me.

_____ 2. I have to wait for the bus or my ride outside, sometimes in the cold.

_____ 3. I get stiff when I have to sit too long.

_____ 4. I'm stiff in the morning, even after I take a warm bath.

_____ 5. I'm stiff in the morning, but I don't have time to take a warm bath before school.

_____ 6. My hands hurt when I write.

___ 7. I can't write fast enough during tests or when taking notes.

___ 8. Writing on the chalkboard is difficult for me.

___ 9. I have trouble raising my hand to ask or answer questions.

___ 10. I sometimes forget to take my splints to school.

___ 11. I don't have the special equipment at school that I need, such as splints, a tilt board, or a wheelchair.

___ 12. It's hard for me to take off my coat, boots, or shoes.

___ 13. It's hard for me to turn door handles or open my locker.

___ 14. It's hard for me to carry my books or lunch tray.

___ 15. I have trouble eating at school.

___ 16. I have trouble using the bathroom at school.

___ 17. I don't have enough time to change classes.

___ 18. My classes, the bathroom, or the cafeteria are too far away for me.

___ 19. Staircases are a problem for me.

___ 20. I have trouble with fire drills or earthquake drills.

___ 21. I have trouble changing my clothes in Physical Education (PE) class.

___ 22. I have trouble taking a shower in PE class.

___ 23. I don't have time to exercise at school.

___ 24. I'm too tired after school to exercise at home.

___ 25. PE is too much for me.

___ 26. My school day is long, and I'm very tired when I get home.

___ 27. I need a rest in the middle of my school day.

___ 28. I have trouble standing in long lines, like in the cafeteria.

___ 29. I have trouble doing all of my homework on time.

___ 30. I can't keep up with the other students in my school work.

___ 31. I'm absent from school a lot (one week or more is a "lot").

___ 32. My school makes me keep my medicine with the school staff.

_____ 33. I sometimes forget to take my medicine at school.

_____ 34. I feel different when I have to go to the office for my medicine.

_____ 35. Some of the other students make fun of my arthritis.

_____ 36. I don't know how to talk to my classmates about my arthritis.

_____ 37. My teacher doesn't understand my arthritis.

_____ 38. My teacher babies me.

_____ 39. My teacher forgets I have arthritis.

As stated in the team care chapter, the majority of teachers are extremely interested in helping if they can, given the time constraints and other students in class. I have found that arthritis is so common among everyone's relatives that most teachers immediately understand the problem it presents on a personal basis. The teacher must have specific written instructions, however, for modifying your child's schedule. You and the teacher must talk it out until you are both comfortable with what needs to be done. Remember to bring the pamphlet, _When Your Student Has Arthritis_ (see Appendix C). Your specific instructions should be in a letter. The following sample letter signed by a mythical student was written by Dr. Beth Ziebell of Tucson, Arizona, and is helpful in illustrating what you need to say and how you need to say it. Your letter must be personal and directly pertain to your child.

Dear Teacher,

I am a child with arthritis and I would like you to know more about me. There are a lot of other kids like me (approximately 250,000 in the United States), but it is possible that because we are spread out all over the 50 states, you may have never had a child with arthritis in your class before.

There are some important things about me that I want to share with you. Sometimes I really hurt, even though there isn't anything wrong with me that you can see. So if I am quiet or withdrawn, it doesn't mean that I'm not interested in school. Mornings can be a problem because my joints can be stiff for the first few hours after I get up and sometimes by late afternoon I feel *tired. A lot of the time I feel really good, but when the arthritis becomes active, I usually feel pretty uncomfortable for a period of time. I hope this will explain why I have up days and down days.*

I want to be in school whenever I can because I know that it is important for my education. I also want to be involved in as many activities and parts of school as I can. Sometimes it might be necessary to work out some special arrangements for me. I can't always take part in the regular playground or physical education programs. Sometimes I have a problem if the distance to the cafeteria or between classes is long or if I have to stand in long lines. I may need to take aspirin during school time because that is a very important part of my treatment for arthritis. And once in a while I may need to leave school for a doctor or physical therapist appointment.

I hope you will have a meeting with me and my folks early in the school year so we can all understand each other better. My Mom and Dad will keep you informed if there are any major changes in my condition during the year that you should know about.

I have the same need for accomplishment and success as all kids. So I want you to have the same expectations for me that you do for all other children. I may be a little slow or awkward but I can do the same things the other kids do if you will just let me. If I can't finish my work in time, please let me take home my assignment instead of excusing me on the grounds that I am handicapped.

Thanks for letting me tell you a little about myself. If you have any other questions, please feel free to ask me or my parents.

Your student,

In writing your letter with the team's help, use the checklist as a guide. Items 1 and 2 are concerned with possible transportation problems. Andrea suggests that if your child must wait for a school bus, try to arrange for her to be picked up in such a way as to avoid standing on a corner in the cold wind or rain. Stiffness is covered in items 3–5. To keep your child from getting stiff, the teacher can let her hand out the papers or erase the board or pick up things at the office to get around a formal getting up every 30 minutes. Sometimes kids with JRA need to prop a leg on a stool or rest after 10 or more minutes of writing.

The next 11 items are concerned with joint motion and pain. Ask your child's teacher to let her use soft plastic pencil grips to help sore fingers, and book holders to reduce the fatigue of holding a book. If possible, see if the teacher will allow your child to keep separate sets of books not only at home but in separate classrooms to reduce the pain of carrying books. If opening a door or locker is a problem, opening aids can be used. If arthritis of the hands prevents taking notes properly, ask if a tape recorder can be used. Be forewarned, however, that asking to use a tape recorder is a real red flag in most schools. Everyone worries about being tape recorded these days. If you encounter a lot of anger or apprehension, let the matter go. It's usually not worth the effort to force the issue. Andrea Kovalesky notes that homework assignments sometimes need to be reduced or permission needs to be given to type them.

Mobility problems (items 17–20) between classes are real for some children. Ask for extra time just before or just after the bell for your child to move between classes to reduce being tripped or slammed into a locker. Here is where you can get into real disagreements with the school over rearranging classes on the same floor or using elevators that do not exist. Ownership of a certain room on a certain floor by a teacher is a real issue. Each room is frequently individualized by the teacher and to broach changing the location of a room for a class to accommodate your child is not possible in most schools. The schoolteachers will quite legitimately feel that you are asking too much to change the location of a particular class to allow greater ease of access for your child. You will need to weigh the need for closer classes with the practicality of asking a teacher to change a classroom for a particular class. The installation of an elevator to solve classroom access problems is not possible given the present financial state of most school systems. Most schools in our country are not user friendly to physically impaired children.

Physical education problems (items 21–25) were discussed in Chapter 5 in the school and exercise section. Go back and read it again. The information is so important that a little repetition is useful. At the end of Appendix C is a copy of an outstanding brochure to help the teacher with PE.

The next five items (26–31) relate to your child's need for rest at school. In my experience, most schools will let your child rest in the school nurse's room during the day, although the team will need to help you get permission. On days when pain and stiffness are so great that your child can't go to school on time, you'll need a flexible program to allow her to arrive late after the stiffness or pain has subsided. The teacher will need to allow your child to make up the period missed without penalty and let your child work at home. You and your child, in turn, must not misuse this privilege. At first glance this arrangement may seem a little Utopian, but I have seen it work time after time—so go for it! The alternative is homebound teaching, which should be avoided if at all possible.

Medication needs (items 32–34) at school must receive close attention. The school needs detailed, written instructions and permission from you to give the medicines to your child. Your child will likely be embarrassed because she'll need to go to the nurse's office to take it. But some schools may have only a part-time nurse or no nurse at all, in which case the ritual is more trouble than it's worth. If at all possible, see if your child can receive her medication at home twice a day so that you can avoid having them given at school. The other kids place such a stigma on those who "take drugs" of any kind that you'll definitely need to work around this one.

The last five items (35–39) are concerned with peer and teacher relationships. Your child may be afraid to tell fellow students, as well as her teacher, that she has a chronic illness and is different. The direct approach is always best—my experience is that when you try to hide an illness, misunderstandings always occur. So broadcast it. Some teachers ask kids with JRA to do show-and-tell talks. Fellow students are fascinated—believe me. Or try to arrange for the Arthritis Foundation's special Kids on the Block puppet show to come to your child's classroom. Everyone loves it, too, even high school students. If the Arthritis Foundation chapter in your town doesn't have a team doing it, organize one yourself and learn puppetry. Remember that a "woe is me" attitude doesn't work around here.

The Law Is on Your Side

Congress has passed laws to help children with special needs in school situations. As a result, special education departments are now standard in school districts. However, my experience is that working one-on-one with the teacher offers the best chance for success. If this approach fails, fall back on the IEP process, which should bring together you and the relevant school personnel to plan your child's educational needs for years to come. In reality, however, many schools are so hard pressed for money and services that the IEP is used as a dodge to deny needed services for your child and thereby get out of paying for them. Unfortunately, many school districts do not regard JRA as part of what they define as special education. If your district understands that JRA is a chronic illness and requires special accommodation, you're in clover. If not, get ready for the fight of your life—but don't give up. Arm yourself with the Arthritis Foundation's manual, *Educational Rights for Children with Arthritis: A Manual for Parents* (see Appendix C).

Using the tools, pamphlets, and ideas in this chapter, you'll be able to move forward in the most important activity of your child's life—education. Having fired you and your family up to work as a team, it's important to remember that JRA must be integrated into your family life and not to let JRA rule your family. The end result of this chapter is the transition to successful adult life. So let's move on to the next chapter.

8

From Juvenile to Adult

Your children are not your children. They are the sons and daughters of Life's longing for itself. They come through you but not from you, and though they are with you yet they belong not to you.

—*The Prophet,* KAHLIL GIBRAN

Welcome to the Real World

The ease with which your child makes the transition from childhood to adulthood is a direct reflection of the time and effort you've spent in preparing her for the future. If she has a positive self-concept, an optimistic outlook, and confidence in her abilities, life will be a lot easier. However, having observed my three children and many, many of their friends without arthritis moving through those years, I have reached a few conclusions. Almost all the youngsters seemed to have difficulty seeing how they would fit into the work force.

I have observed the most charming, intelligent young people filled with incredible self-doubt. Their lack of confidence in their ability to be assimilated into the working world has rendered me speechless. After some thought I have concluded that they are intimidated by looking only at the end result rather than at the small steps necessary to get them there.

The anecdote I used with my own children is from my garden in Houston. We had about three-quarters of an acre of heavily landscaped land to maintain. In the spring I would have a large dump truck filled with mulch delivered, another with topsoil, and another with 50-pound bags of fertilizer. My children, in their early teens, were absolutely overwhelmed. "How in the world are you going to spread all that stuff, mom?" Indeed, it was rather intimidating to look at those mountains of dirt. But my reply was always, "One wheelbarrow at a time!" Isn't that what life is all about? One step at a time, one shovel at a time, one block to build on?

The wonderful violinist Itzhak Perlman once spoke to a group of handicapped children. Having had polio as a child, his legs are pretty much useless. After dragging his body across the room using his crutches, with the children in observant silence, he sat down to a very attentive audience. He looked at the children and said, "OK, we all know what doesn't work. Now, let's see what does work." He picked up his violin and began to play his magic. No one doubted what worked!

If you have a child who has had to cope with arthritis, he or she is probably a lot tougher in many respects than the average child. On every level this child has had to face things that most children never imagine. The children with rheumatic diseases I have met have been impressive in their determination, their resilience, their maturity. As a parent you need to point out, repeatedly, the merits of all the courage they have had to muster in order to get to the point where they are now. They probably don't realize just how difficult the path has been, and just how much strength they have had to demonstrate. Remind them!

At the age of 15, Elizabeth began taking gold injections twice a week, and if she missed one she began to have problems. Her life pretty much revolved around those injections. The summer after her junior year of high school she had the opportunity to take a fantastic trip to Europe for six weeks with some of her classmates. Of course, a major consideration was how to continue the injections uninterrupted. She was embarrassed to ask one of the teachers to give them to her. So she went to Earl and asked him if he would teach her to give them to herself. His reaction demonstrated a great deal of faith in this 16-year-old. He scratched his head a few times, rubbed his chin, looked at his nurse, and said, "Why not?" And he then proceeded to do so. This was not my idea and personally I could never watch her do it. Obviously the trip meant enough to her to overcome her fear of giving herself these intramuscular injections. Ouch!

Field hockey was one of the sports in high school that Elizabeth would have liked very much to participate in. Admitting to herself that it was impossible, she became the team manager. She had fun and shared the camaraderie of her friends and was there to cheer the team on. Learning to compromise in life, to change the game plan when it's not working, is a very important part of growing up.

I have faith in the ability of these children to face the corporate world and to succeed as well as any other group of young adults. They have navigated the world of medicine. They have seen the public's ignorance. They have a level of maturity that many adults never achieve.

Let's Concentrate on What Works!

Over the past 12 years, Earl and I have compared notes about different children with arthritis and their families. I would separate them into two categories. There are parents who get lost in the "poor little you" trap. Other parents accept the situation and begin to look for solutions with their child. When pity is the predominant emotion a child receives, she will probably behave in a pitiful manner. But if a child is honestly praised for her real effort, she will probably behave in a praiseworthy manner. As a parent you have to be diligent in your efforts, despite the emotional pain you feel, to encourage your child to be positive. In the business world a "poor little me" attitude will not get you very far.

I know that most young adults with arthritis make an effort to conceal the fact from their employer. Depending on the severity of the disease, they may or may not be able to pull it off. I think our society is slowly changing its attitude toward people with impairments in the workplace. Your child will have to decide on her own whether or not she can handle it. If she is confident of her abilities she can probably face the situation. I know that Elizabeth decided very early that everyone she knew had problems; hers just happened to be arthritis and it was visible. Some of her friends had much more serious problems, even if they weren't as visible.

Many parents have told me that when their children moved from one area of their lives to another, for example from high school to college, they made a concerted effort not to let anyone know they had arthritis. Some of these young people have very obvious problems related to arthritis. I have never been sure just how they handle the situation, what they tell their new friends. And in personal relationships honesty is not only the best policy, it is the only policy. Unfortunately, I know of more than a few romantic relationships that were abruptly ended when the other person found out about the arthritis, but in that case your daughter is better off without him. When you begin dating it is preferable to be completely honest in the beginning of the relationship about your arthritis since it is there and it is a reality. Would you try to hide your religious preference? The fact that you are Italian (or Irish, or German)? Sooner or later this person will find out about these facts. If they can't accept it you are much better off knowing that early on, before you become seriously involved. One young lady I know took her fiancé to visit her new rheumatologist. She asked the doctor to explain everything she knew about this nasty disease: possible prognosis, medications and side effects, effects during pregnancy, the possibility of passing the disease on to children. They are now happily married.

Earl will address some of the situations that arise when your child must change from a pediatric physician to an adult physician, and try to help you make it a smooth transition. However, if your child has been treated by a pediatric rheumatologist and a health team, it really is severing a very close tie. The team members become like a part of your extended family. They are familiar with your history, your problems, and your successes. The members of Earl's health team, which we referred to as the A-Team, became our friends. We were fighting a common enemy—arthritis.

I know one young lady, with a very thick medical chart, who had to move on to the adult rheumatologist. She presented the chart to the new physician and made herself comfortable in a chair opposite the doctor. As the new doctor thumbed through the chart she periodically looked up at the patient. When she finished she looked at the girl and said, "I don't know why you're not in a wheelchair!" Fighting back the tears, she told the doctor that indeed she knew why she was not in a wheelchair. It was because of very aggressive medical treatment, extensive physical therapy, occupational therapy, a lot of guidance, and just plain *guts*.

Even though my thoughts on this subject might step on a few toes, you need to understand that many adult rheumatologists are different in their approach to care, and you need to find one who fits your child's needs. I had a wonderful friend, Helga, who developed rheumatoid arthritis in her mid-30s. Helga began going to a rheumatologist in the medical center. About the only thing her physician did was prescribe medications and dismiss her with, "If you have a problem call me." He did not explain the disease process to her, possible side effects of the medication, what to expect on a daily basis, or anything else.

Helga had observed the battle we had been fighting to keep Elizabeth going. She had suffered along with me and now she found herself in the same struggle. When she had a question she would call me, not wanting to "impose on her doctor," and she wasn't quite sure what he considered a problem. Was not being able to get out of bed in the morning a problem? (Give me a break!) She didn't understand why she was so fatigued, why she was so cold much of the time. She had been very active, but involved in all the wrong activities for a person with arthritis. She wanted to know what kind of exercises she should be doing. Someone needed to plan a physical therapy program for her, including swimming. She needed someone who understood how imperative education is in the management of this chronic disease. First, I hope you will find a pediatric rheumatologist to give your child the very best care. Then I hope your child is fortunate enough to outgrow the arthritis before adulthood. And if not, I hope when the time comes to change to an adult rheumatologist you will look carefully for a physician who will treat the whole person and not just the disease. The difference could mean a great deal to the quality of your child's life.

Earl's Advice

The first seven chapters of this book have been leading up to this one. All of our advice about positive attitudes, hard work, proper coordination of services, and a good education bring us to the real bottom line: your child will grow up. In the process she must receive a decent education, obtain a decent job, and have sufficient maturity, as well as make enough money, to live independently. Your expectations and attitude are critical here. If you expect something from your child, you'll get something. If you don't, you won't. Here, in a nutshell, is this chapter's message.

A Harris survey and several other surveys have found that a large percentage of disabled young adults are jobless even though they want to work. If you happen to be well off, don't sit there smugly in your chair thinking that your child will be immune, as children of upper-income families are sidelined as often as children of poor families are. I realize I've already said that three of four children with JRA have little or no functional impairment as adults, so you may be wondering what the big deal is. Well, despite the relatively good physical shape they're in, very few kids with JRA have anything approaching the work experience of their non-JRA peers. Dr. Pacey White at the National Children's Medical Center in Washington, D.C., discovered that most of her teenage JRA patients not only did not hold a part-time job but had never held a job.

Dr. White studied about a hundred chronically ill adolescents of all kinds, ages 12 to 16 years, and found them to be vocationally immature compared to other early teenagers. When actual work experience of these kids was examined, they were way behind the norm. Even more to the point, it didn't matter whether their parents earned their living as doctors or clerks. It also didn't matter whether their disability was severe or mild.

So what was the determining factor? Parental expectations—or the lack of them. The parents of the kids in the study said that they didn't expect their children to work until 16 or so. Most teenagers with no disabilities are at least baby-sitting, mowing the lawn, or doing volunteer work by that point.

Now that I've hit you over the head with data and percentages, you know enough to treat your child differently. Begin to *expect* something from her by the age of 10. The best way for her to learn a work ethic is to work at home first and then to work for someone else. Keep in mind that we're talking about Saturday cleanup jobs, not working the night shift in a coal mine.

The next thing is to teach your daughter to tell an employer that her disability is an asset. Instead, many parents teach their children to lie to potential employers about having arthritis. That works, but I like Dr. White's approach better. She runs yearly job awareness programs in which local employers participate. The program also provides teens with telephone consultation and referrals, a career library, job readiness, and career exploration sessions. This approach is really new, but it's well worth your while to persuade your child's center to get with it.

The Texas Vocational Rehabilitation Commission has assigned two counselors in Houston to work with chronically ill students from 12 years on to help them with job attitudes and planning. I'm sure that there are many other similar programs, but you're going to have to find them—or organize one yourself.

Making the Break—Changing to an Adult Rheumatologist

She's old enough, out of school, has a job, is off your insurance (if you still have any for her), and has her own place. She may or may not have her own significant or indispensable other. The last time you went to the doctor, the new team nurse noted that your daughter was older than she was. Believe it or not, this is a fairly routine story for JRA kids after college or school. Let's face it: at some point the knowledge of the pediatrician is no longer better than that of the adult doctor. The trick is for the teenager or young adult, parent, and physician to recognize together when to change doctors and to plan the transition carefully from the team to an adult rheumatologist or internist.

There are plenty of good reasons to make the change. For one, continued care by the pediatric team is cumbersome when your child is too old to be admitted to a children's hospital. In that case, the team has to try to work in an adult hospital or in a wing of adult patients.

Of course, after a child, parents, and physician have been down the trail together for so many years, it's tough to change. The bond of friendship and trust is so strong that a new physician seems like an interloper. In addition, adult rheumatologists have firm beliefs about relating to patients. They feel strongly that your child needs to break the umbilical cord to Mother. What does that mean? It means that they don't want you coming to the doctor with a grown-up child. They want to deal exclusively with her and consider all information about her care confidential—in other words, beyond your reach, unless your child chooses to tell you. They are correct that we need to develop the independence of JRA kids in the teenage years by having them go to the office alone and depending on them to relay information to their parents. It's true that from ages 10 to 12 we ask you to begin giving your child responsibility for taking her medicine. The internist's big beef with us as pediatricians is that we molly coddle kids with JRA far too long and need to jolt them into maturity. Many feel that a team is only a dodge to create family dependency on the doctor. My own rule is that by the age of 30 at the latest, all JRA kids should be seeing an adult doctor.

Making the Change

After everyone agrees that it's time for your child to change from a team to an adult doctor, the old doctor should call or visit the new doctor, records in hand, to discuss the patient. I've also asked the new physician to come to the clinic to meet patients and their families with the team present. Some parents make an appointment with the adult doctor and visit with him. The biggest difference you will notice in working with a new doctor is the absence of a team. With few exceptions, the adult doctors work alone except for a nurse assistant. Above all, don't try the "cold turkey" treatment of sudden change—just making an appointment with no orderly changeover period is too "cold turkey." More often than not you'll go back to the team with tears in your eyes. This, of course, helps the ego of the old doc and the rest of the team but doesn't help you make the changeover.

Even after the change has occurred, a few visits by you and your now adult child to the old team are helpful to establish rapport better with the new physician and his way of doing things. Kathy already addressed the issue of stressful experiences with a new physician from a patient's and parent's view.

The major goal is to have a smooth changing of the guard with full communication between the team, new doc, patient, and parent. If things are not going well, speak up and solve the problems before someone gets mad. With JRA young adults or teenagers with significant problems this is a critical issue. This is the time for all concerned to focus on what is best for the patient—and not to worry about egos on either side. Another way to look at it, however, is, isn't it nice that so many people care?

Finding the Right College or Trade School

Of course you've agonized over whether your child's SAT or ACT is high enough to get her into that special school. The school counselor has ticked you off by pushing her favorite schools, ones you've never heard of—and your daughter has told you that she will not go to one of those all-girls schools or the state university, where the fees are affordable. Welcome to the club. The only milestone equivalent to sending your child to college is planning her wedding.

Here's a tip that I didn't know until a year or so ago. It may help you a lot. If your child has arthritis of the hands or gets too stiff sitting for the time required for the SAT, PSAT, or ACT, you can make an application before she takes it the first time and get an untimed test that will help ease the rush to finish properly if the fingers are too tired and painful. Do it!

As you and your child consider different schools, one thing you need to determine right off the bat is whether the college towns that interest you are large enough to have an experienced rheumatologist. Find out after you've narrowed down your field of schools. Once your child has decided where she wants to go, ask your home team to contact the doctor in town to establish rapport. Also, ask the team to send reports to the school health service, although most such services are not set up to handle chronic illnesses. You can't expect them to know everything about everything.

If your child has physical limitations, it's also important to check whether the school is disability friendly, with lots of elevators and ramps at curbs and into buildings.

In some states, it pays to see whether your vocational rehabilitation services will help your child with college tuition or other expenses. It's a long shot, but many of the families in our center have been helped this way. Be sure to check the scholarships at the college where your child wants to go. You can find odd and unusual scholarships in some places, including a few for the disabled. A number of books listing scholarships are available at public libraries, and I urge you to review them. My own brother, a Ph.D. in economic American history and president of a large college in Denver, paid for his undergraduate degree in history at the University of Texas with a scholarship for Texas residents who could prove that they had forebears who lived in the South during the Civil War. Tom traveled to Mississippi and found that the courthouse with all of the records had burned after the war, but with the help of a family Bible, he was able to win the scholarship.

We've had several children go off to college in our family, and we've fought the battle of whether to take those expensive courses to get a better score on the SAT. Some took the courses, and some did not. I think the instruction focuses the student on how important it is to do as well as possible, and if nothing else, it helps in that way. Also, don't let anyone snow you and say that the tests are unimportant to getting in—nonsense! They look at high school class standing, scores, and recommendations. If your grandfather gives a few million, that definitely helps.

Be sure to tell them that your daughter has JRA. Many schools try to take a certain percentage of children with special needs, and her JRA may make her a more desirable candidate rather than a less desirable one.

Planning the Future

The basic message of this book, as you've surmised by now, is upbeat and positive. However, we do need to talk about a downbeat word, "the I word," *insurance*, both health and life.

Health Insurance

Hopefully the health insurance and health care problems in our country will be resolved by the time your child enters the job market. Right now, the cost of health insurance is accelerating at the rate of 10 to 25 percent yearly. The cost is now so large a part of employee expenses that it may be difficult for your child to find employment in a small company that needs to keep insurance costs down. It makes the most sense for JRA kids to prepare to work in a large corporation or public entity. Individual health insurance for JRA kids, or even those with a history of JRA or any other kind of arthritis, now is basically unobtainable or so expensive that it is impractical.

Understanding the constant changes in health insurance rules and practices in the United States is much like trying to put up road signs in Galveston Bay. Neither one makes any sense. With 1,500 insurance plans and no overarching system, it's incredible that anything works. You've probably already discovered certain ground rules, but I'll repeat them anyway: *JRA* is a buzzword to insurance carriers. At the first opportunity most companies will discontinue your policy if at all possible. If you change or lose your job, the new carrier will undoubtedly disallow your child's JRA for coverage. If you're lucky, the insurance carrier will only disallow JRA expenses. This has the effect of freezing you or your spouse in a given job, hoping against hope that you don't get fired or the company doesn't go out of business. The picture isn't always this dark, of course. If you're one of the lucky ones who works for Exxon or another large company, you're in great shape.

Another problem you must face is coverage after your child goes off your health insurance following her graduation from school. A few companies write health insurance for JRAs, but very few. The premiums are often too expensive for most to afford, particularly young adults trying to get started in life. The penalty by the insurance carriers is totally unjustified because the usual JRA young adult does not have large medical fees and has been in remission for many years.

If you have received financial help from a state Title V program (in Texas it is called Chronically and Disabled Children's Services), these funds also stop at adulthood. The age varies from state to state. In general there is no continuation of funds after legal maturity of your child. There is an excellent monograph by Julie Beckett, *Health Care Financing: A Guide for Families*, written for the Federal Maternal and Child Health Bureau. Be sure to consult this, as it lists and explains services available state by state and gives the addresses of many agencies. You can obtain a copy by writing to the following address: National Maternal and Child Health Research Center, College of Law Building, University of Iowa, Iowa City, IA 52242.

Life Insurance

Read carefully here. At the present time, no matter how mild your child's JRA is or has become, life insurance will be either impossible or almost impossible to obtain. At some point, someone will persuade life insurance actuaries that JRA or indeed arthritis in children does not lead to significant loss of life or early death. You and I know that; the insurance carriers don't. As with health insurance, a few carriers write life insurance policies, but very few. They generally write it as a high-risk policy. This becomes important for young adults with jobs and children. If you can lock in some permanent life insurance in your child's name with your employee plan or your spouse's, do so now for as much as you can afford.

Afterword

Hope for the Future

I had observed firsthand the tremendous effort needed to maintain our family, my sanity, communication with the medical community, communication with the school, and have normal relationships with friends and relatives during the difficult days of my daughter's illness. So I was delighted in 1984 when Earl asked me to help him organize the First Annual American Juvenile Arthritis Organization (AJAO) Conference. The AJAO is a coalition of health professionals, parents, children with various rheumatic diseases, and anyone interested in improving the quality of life for children with JRA.

Earl explained that it would be a two- or three-day conference, held at a resort. The primary focus was on the family and how it copes with various rheumatic diseases, since it is indeed a family battle. Parents, children with a rheumatic disease, siblings, and other family members would participate. The idea was to find out what the families needed and gather resources to help them. We would invite the health professionals who care for children with rheumatic diseases, including physicians, nurses, physical therapists, occupational therapists, nutritionists, and psychologists. All of this would be under the auspices of the Arthritis Foundation, based in Atlanta, Georgia. Also contributing enormously was the Department of Maternal and Child Health in Washington, D.C.

The concept was unique to me. Having been married to a physician for many years, I had not heard of a meeting where physicians,

125

patients, and families could gather to share experiences and learn from one another. Most of the medical meetings I had observed were doctor to doctor, oriented around the problems of acutely ill patients. When you are dealing with a chronic illness, you can't simply take care of the problem and move on to the next one. Without collaboration between health professionals and families, care becomes sporadic and ineffective. I was absolutely delighted with the idea of the conference as a means of establishing communication between all the concerned parties.

At that time the AJAO was only a few years old and looking for its identity. A small group of parents had convinced the Arthritis Foundation that there was a need for a parent's organization. Dawn Hafeli, from Detroit, was one of those parents. She has been a very positive force and, as a matter of fact, is now working full time for the AJAO. Dr. Frank Donivan from Washington, DC, is another friend who has been an inspiration. If I listed all the people who have impacted the direction of the AJAO, we would have another book. Suffice it to say that there are many dedicated people who have made the AJAO the great group that it is today.

Another motivating factor for me was the tremendous ignorance in the public sector about juvenile rheumatic diseases. Elizabeth was continually explaining to people that the reason she limped so badly was that she had arthritis, only to hear them exclaim, "But arthritis is what *old* people get!" But arthritis afflicts up to 250,000 children. The quality of life for many children is dramatically diminished, and most people have no idea it is happening.

Earl suggested that I, as a parent and lay person, write a letter to all the families of children with rheumatic diseases that we could identify in the country through the Arthritis Foundation and the Regional Pediatric Rheumatology Centers. I explained the concept of the meeting and asked for the families' suggestions as to the subjects they would like to cover in those three days. The response was remarkable.

I received letters from every area of the country. Families told of children struggling for many years without ever meeting another child with the same problem. Many were confined to wheelchairs. Many were obviously not getting adequate medical care. Many described serious problems with school systems. Parents told of the struggle to maintain a semblance of normal family life.

At that time I had a mailbox about 150 feet from my front door. I would go out to get the mail and usually open it on the walk back to the house. Many of these letters were so filled with pain that I frequently returned to the house in tears. If there was any doubt about the necessity for this conference it disappeared with each letter. And with each letter my resolve to help was intensified.

Armed with these letters from the families, Earl and I went to the Executive Committee meeting of the AJAO in Denver in the winter of 1984. There was some disagreement about how or whether to proceed with the national conference. After the members read the letters I had received, we voted to move ahead with the project.

With input from the executive committee, the families who had written to me, and the health team from Texas Children's Hospital, we organized the format for the First Annual Meeting of the AJAO. It immediately became clear that we would never run out of topics for discussion. The initial ideas that flowed from all the sources would have needed five meetings to cover completely. I typed the program, with descriptions of each session, and photocopied the six pages. Then I threw a pizza party and prepared the mailing with the help of my daughter's friends. They were wonderful! I think it gave them a sense of doing something to help Elizabeth. I know they suffered with her in those years.

There were some considerable hurdles to overcome to organize this first meeting. We did not have much time and speakers had to be contacted by phone instead of mail. Funds were short and had to be gathered from several different sources. The Bureau of Maternal and Child Health in Washington allowed us to bring speakers to Keystone with funds already in their grants. A family in Argentina, whose child had been successfully treated by Earl, donated $1,000 to the cause. And a few other sympathetic souls pitched in to help. There were "doubting Thomases" who did not think that anyone would come to the meeting. But it was because they did not understand how parents feel when they see their child suffering daily with a chronic illness. They did not realize that you will literally "fight tigers" to help her. Besides, I truly felt that if one family came to the conference, I would consider it a success.

I am happy to report that 250 people flocked to Keystone, Colorado, that July. They came from 25 states, Canada, and Australia. We had planned an opening reception on a patio outdoors. Fate would have it that a storm swept over the Rockies at that exact hour, and we had to move the dinner inside. I think God watches out for His children. Because we were all strangers and a little awkward, forcing us into a smaller space created interesting dynamics. Within an hour the older children had gravitated to a corner room in the restaurant. Crutches and wheelchairs had been discarded against a wall, conversation was lively, and new friendships had begun to form. Viewing this from across the room, I knew that this was what all the effort had been about. Earl came up beside me, took me by the elbow, and led me to a window. He pointed out toward the sky. The storm had passed, and there was the most magnificent double rainbow radiating across the valley. An auspicious beginning!

One particularly exceptional young man attended that first meeting in Keystone. Benjamin Horgan was 14 years old and living in Australia. He had learned about the meeting from a newsletter sent out by the Arthritis Foundation. He immediately called Qantas Airlines and asked if they would fly him and his mother to the meeting for free, of course! The airline people were so taken by Ben's enthusiasm and charm that they agreed not only to fly them to Colorado, but to include a stop at Disneyland! He also called some of the service organizations in Sydney and secured financial assistance from them.

When Benjamin and his mother, Barbara, came to Keystone, he was in a wheelchair. Several physicians had told them that the damage to Ben's joints was so extensive he would not be able to walk until he stopped growing and joint replacements could be performed. Ben was determined to make the best of it. I still remember looking out a window to see him pull out a water gun he had hidden in the wheelchair, and shooting an unsuspecting nurse. He was irrepressible!

The following year a most extraordinary thing happened. Ben came to the second annual meeting in St. Louis. He was WALKING! In an interview conducted by a local television crew, he said he had observed so many other children at the previous meeting who could walk, that he went home with a new resolve. He began to swim and exercise with weights. He told his mother that if he dropped anything she should just leave it where it fell. If he wanted it badly enough he would manage to retrieve it. What a wonderful spirit! What courage!

I wish I could relate this story to every physician who treats children and every parent who is struggling to encourage their child. Be careful about placing limits on your developing child. Maybe running is impossible for your child at a certain point in time, but it may not be forever. If you tell children they can't, in all probability they won't. Give your child encouragement and support. If she can't do something because of the disease, I assure you that it will become painfully self-evident very rapidly.

At our third AJAO meeting in Los Angeles, a woman about 60 years old, in a wheelchair, participated in a small group session with me. A friend of hers was at the meeting with her. He helped her get around and also participated in the meeting. I was very curious as to why this older person would want to attend a children's meeting. She explained to me that she had developed the disease at a very young age. She had been given heavy doses of steroids as a child, back when they were viewed as the miracle cure. Now she was a very tiny person, seriously disabled.

Born in the Midwest in a very conservative community, this woman became ill at a very young age. Her parents were helpless to understand what was happening. In their ignorance, sense of guilt, and pain, they kept her in bed. She was literally locked in her room, the shame of her family. At the age of 45 she began to understand, from watching television and reading, that California was a much freer society, that they viewed the disabled differently, and that they had wonderful social services. She ran away from home at the age of 45. My mind reeled at the thought of a woman of 45, in a wheelchair, running away from home. Go west, indeed! She explained that she had come to our conference because she was so delighted that something was finally being done to help the whole child and the whole family. She wanted to let parents know how much conditions have improved for children with chronic illness, that things are indeed improving, that the future is so much brighter for the new generation of children with arthritis.

I made reference earlier to the fact that there were people who could not see the reason for holding a national conference or for inviting the children to participate. Since the first annual meeting of the AJAO in 1984, each successive meeting has reinforced my initial feelings. These meetings are in fact contributing to improving the quality of life for children with JRA. We need each other. We need the communication engendered by these encounters.

I had worked so hard to make the first meeting a reality. I will never forget the first morning of the meeting. It was a spectacular day, as you will only find in the Rocky Mountains on a summer morning after a storm the evening before. The sun was brilliant, the air was fresh and crisp, the river was gurgling by us on its way downstream. I was approaching the meeting room to begin the first day of the first conference. The world looked terrific to me. I saw a little boy from Houston, eight-year-old Joey, by the river in his wheelchair. He flagged me down with such enthusiasm I had to stop. With his eyes gleaming he showed me the rocks he had collected to take home to his older brother. With a hug around the neck he thanked me for bringing them all here for the meeting and he commented on how beautiful it was.

Before I reached the meeting room, several mothers stopped me to complain. Their consensus was that it was horrible to bring children to such a beautiful place when they would never be able to ski. I stood there with my mouth open. I thought, "Gee, it's summer. Who's skiing?" and, "I broke my foot five years ago skiing. I guess I may never ski again either." But I have to tell you that I really love being in the mountains. My message would be to give your child a sketching pad and pencils if they can't ski. Teach them to draw those magnificent mountains. Collect rocks by the river. Inhale the wonderful fresh air. Go hot-air ballooning. Enjoy life. Find the things you CAN do! By this point we all know what doesn't work. Let's find out what DOES work. It is so important to guide our children to activities that will enhance the quality of their lives. Elizabeth can't play tennis. But she takes the most beautiful photographs. Most children, when faced with the inability to do certain activities, almost always find new, previously untapped resources. They have talents they were never aware of sitting in front of a television. But they need our encouragement, our enthusiasm, our guidance.

The annual AJAO conferences bring these young people together to share their experiences and it is a tremendous learning experience for all. They learn that they are not alone. Their parents learn that they have a lot to share with the other parents. Health professionals come to share their knowledge with us, and more importantly, they learn what it is like to live with arthritis. Instead of seeing a patient for an hour in a treatment room, they see how a day in the life of a child with arthritis is different. The day moves a little slower if you are in a wheelchair, if you have splints on, if you can't zip up your blue jeans, if you are sick from your medication, or if you have to take time out for peritoneal dialysis.

This kind of mutual understanding has generated so many wonderful things. Educational materials which are so helpful to the families have been initiated because of these meetings. Children have come away with a renewed sense of self-esteem. Parents have learned that the crazy quilt of feelings they have about their child are absolutely normal. Health professionals have realized the tremendous positive impact they have on the lives of so many families. Public awareness is increasing. We have the opportunity to impact public policy. These meetings present opportunities to begin reconstructing the balance of the family mobile if it was, indeed, damaged by the onset and process of the disease.

Joining the AJAO is a positive thing *you* can do. The organization has a newsletter that will keep you informed about current treatments and other pertinent information for families. I believe very strongly in becoming an activist when faced with adversity. From time to time there are issues before the Congress which may affect people with arthritis. If you are aware of them you can write letters and call your congressman. In the case of sometimes sweeping legislation, ignorance is NOT bliss. If a new law is going to affect you, you have the right and obligation to comment. There are serious questions about obtaining insurance coverage, for example. If your child were to need joint replacements in the future and could not get insurance, you would have a serious problem. You need to be informed about all these happenings. Become involved with the Arthritis Foundation.

There is still an enormous amount of work to do: improving patient and family education, increasing public awareness and governmental awareness, training more pediatric rheumatologists and health professionals to treat our children. Outreach clinics need to be established to serve children in rural areas. Funds must be raised to accomplish all of this, but mostly, funds are needed in order to conduct the research to find a cure for these nasty diseases.

You can make a difference. As a parent of a child with arthritis, whose grandmother and aunt had the same disease, I know that there is a possibility that in the future my grandchildren may develop arthritis. I want this awful disease to be conquered by the time they arrive. I know that you do, too. And you will feel much better by doing something positive to help. Join us in the fight!

Appendix A

List of
Pediatric Rheumatologists

The following list includes pediatric rheumatologists who are members of either the Rheumatology Section of the American Academy of Pediatrics or the Pediatric Rheumatology Section of the American College of Rheumatology. We have made every effort to be complete, but it may pay to check with your physician to learn whether there are additional pediatric rheumatologists in your area.

ARIZONA

C. C. DeBenedetti, M.D.
245 Canyon View Drive
Tucson, AZ 85704

ARKANSAS

Betty A. Lowe, M.D.
Arkansas Children's Hospital
800 Marshall Street
Little Rock, AR 72202-3591

CALIFORNIA

Bram Bernstein, M.D.
Division of Rheumatology
Children's Hospital of Los Angeles
4650 Sunset Boulevard
Los Angeles, CA 90027

Niels E. Brandstrup, M.D.
Children's Hospital at Stanford
2500 Hospital Drive, Bldg. 12
Mountain View, CA 94040-4106

Nancy P. Cummings, M.D.
1300 Crane Street
Menlo Park, CA 94025

Nancy E. Doyle, M.D.
1200 Sonoma Ave.
Santa Rosa, CA 95405

Helen M. Emery, M.D.
University of California, San Francisco
505 Parnassus Ave, Box 0105
San Francisco, CA 94143

Virgil Hanson, M.D.
Children's Hospital of Los Angeles
4650 Sunset Boulevard
Los Angeles, CA 90027

Michael Hendrickson
Valley Children's Hospital
3481 E. Shields
Fresno, CA 93726

Albert R. Katz, M.D.
5363 Balboa Boulevard, Suite 445
Encino, CA 91316

Karen K. King, M.D.
Children's Hospital of Los Angeles
4650 Sunset Blvd.
Los Angeles, CA 90027-6016

George N. Lockie, M.D.
1001 E. Grand Avenue
Escondido, CA 92025

Deborah K. McCurdy, M.D.
Children's Hospital of Orange County
455 S. Main Street
Orange, CA 92668

John Miller, M.D., Ph.D.
Children's Hospital at Stanford
520 Sand Hill Road
Palo Alto, CA 94304

Louise E. Sanematsu
Children's Hospital of Orange County
55 South Main
Orange, CA 92668

Christy I. Sanborg, M.D.
Children's Hospital of Orange County
455 South Main
Orange, CA 92668

Elizabeth Smithwick, M.D.
UC Davis Medical Center
Department of Pediatrics
4301 X Street
Sacramento, CA 95817

Dennis O. Stobie, M.D.
Stockton Kaiser-Permanente
PO Box 21005
Stockton, CA 95269-9005

Ilone S. Szer, M.D.
Children's Hospital of San Diego
3030 Children's Way #202
San Diego, CA 92123

Diana Wara, M.D.
University of California, San Francisco
505 Parnassus Avenue, M-679
San Francisco, CA 94143

Robert D. Watson, M.D.
Medical Clinic of Sacramento
3160 Folsom Boulevard
Sacramento, CA 95816

Michael J. Welch, M.D.
3444 Kearny Villa Road, #10
San Diego, CA 92123

COLORADO

B. Dorion
National Jewish Center
1400 Jackson Street, K1026
Denver, CO 80206

Terri Finkel
Children's Hospital
1056 E 19th Street
Denver, CO 80218J

Roger Hollister
Children's Hospital
1056 E 19th Street
Denver, CO 80218

Susan Tiegs
National Jewish Center
1400 Jackson Street, K1026
Denver, CO 80206

CONNECTICUT

Paul L. McCarthy, M.D., Ph.D.
Section of Rheumatology
Yale Medical School
333 Cedar Street
New Haven, CT 06510

Lawrence Zemel, M.D.
Department of Pediatric Rheumatology
Newington Children's Hospital
181 E. Cedar Street
Newington, CT 06111

DELAWARE

Robert A. Doughty, M.D.
Alfred I. DuPont Institute
P.O. Box 269
1600 Rockland Road
Wilmington, DE 19899

Carlos Rose
Alfred I. DuPont Institute
1600 Rockefeller Road
Wilmington, DE 19899

DISTRICT OF COLUMBIA

Ellen Goldmuntz
Department of Pediatric Rheumatology
Children's National Medical Center
111 Michigan Avenue, N.W.
Washington, DC 20016

Robert Lipnick, M.D.
Department of Rheumatology
Children's Hospital Medical Center
111 Michigan Avenue, N.W.
Washington, DC 20010

S. Ray Mitchell
Section on Rheumatology
Georgetown University Medical Center
3800 Reservoir Road, N.W.
Washington, DC 20007

Patience White, M.D.
Department of Pediatric Rheumatology
Children's National Medical Center
111 Michigan Avenue, N.W.
Washington, DC 20010

Karyl Sue Barron, M.D.
Department of Pediatric Rheumatology
Children's National Medical Center
111 Michigan Avenue, N.W.
Washington, DC 20010

FLORIDA

Jose Andrade, M.D.
5412 Curry Ford Road
Orlando, FL 32812

Robert W. Nickeson, Jr.
Diagnostic Clinic
3131 McMullen Booth Road
Clearwater, FL 34621

Rafael F. Rivas-Chacon
Miami Children's Hosptal
6125 S.W. 31st Street
Miami, FL 33155-3098

Mandel R. Sher, M.D.
9555 Seminole Boulevard, Suite 202
Seminole, FL 34642

GEORGIA

Donna Gibbas, M.D.
Century Circle, Suite 14
Atlanta, GA 30345

Rita Jerath
Dept. of Pediatrics
Medical College of Georgia
CJ117
Augusta, GA 30912-0001

Larry B. Vogler
Emory University School of Medicine
2040 Ridgewood Drive
Atlanta, GA 30322-110

HAWAII

David K. Kurahara
Kapilani Med Center for Women
1319 Punahou Street, Suite 734
Honolulu, HI 96826

Col. Donald Person, M.D.
Department of Pediatrics
Tripler Army Medical Center
Honolulu, HI 96859-5000

ILLINOIS

Susan Jay, M.D.
Loyola University Medical Center
Department of Pediatrics
2160 S. First Avenue, Room 4671
Maywood, IL 60180

David R. Keim
Beaumont Clinic
1821 S. Webster
Green Bay IL 54301

Marisa S. Klein-Gitelman
Children's Memorial Hospital
2300 Children's Plaza
Chicago, IL 60614-2620

Robert L. Levy, M.D.
400 County Line Road
Deerfield, IL 60015

Michael Miller
Children's Memorial Hospital
2300 Children's Plaza
Chicago, IL 60614-2620

Lauren Pachman, M.D.
Children's Memorial Hospital
Immuno/Rheumatology
2300 Children's Plaza
Chicago, IL 60614

Kenneth C. Rich, M.D.
Department of Pediatrics
University of Illinois
840 S. Wood Street
Chicago, IL 60612

Paul R. Scholl
Children's Memorial Hospital
2300 Children's Plaza
Chicago, IL 60614-2620

Charles Spencer, M.D.
Division of Pediatric Rheumatology
La Rabida, University of Chicago
E. 65th Street at Lake Michigan
Chicago, IL 60649

Susan Tiegs, M.D.
La Rabida Children's Hospital
East 65th at Lake Michigan
Chicago, IL 60649

Linda Wagner-Weiner
Pediatric Rheumatology
LaRabida Hospital
E. 65th at Lake Michigan
Chicago, IL 60649

INDIANA

Susan H. Ballinger
Riley Hospital for Children
702 Rarnhill Dr. Rm. 5863
Indianapolis, IN 46260-5225

Suzanne Bowyer, M.D.
Riley Hospital for Children
702 Barnhill Drive
Indianapolis, IN 46202

IOWA

Mary M. Jones, M.D.
Pediatric Rheumatology
University of Iowa Hospital & Clinic
Iowa City, IA 52242

KANSAS

Carol Lindsley, M.D.
Department of Pediatrics
Division of Rheumatology
University of Kansas Medical Center
Kansas City, KS 66103

Nancy Olson, M.D.
University of Kansas Medical School
38th and Rainbow Boulevard
Kansas City, KS 66103

KENTUCKY

Richard Mier
Shriner's Hospital
1900 Richmond Road
Lexington, KY 40502-1298

Kenneth N. Schikler, M.D.
Kosair Children's Hospital
200 E. Chestnut Street
Louisville, KY 40202

LOUISIANA

Abraham Gedalia, M.D.
Department of Pediatrics
LSU Medical Center
1542 Tulane Avenue
New Orleans, LA 70112

MARYLAND

Ildy M. Katona
Pediatrics\USUHS
4301 Jones Bridge Road
Bethesda, MD 20814

Robert Lipnick
Pediatrics\USUHS
4301 Jones Bridge Road
Bethesda, MD 20814

Edward M. Sills, M.D.
The Johns Hopkins Hospital
600 N. Wolfe Street
Baltimore, MD 21205-2182

Carolyn Yancey
Cigna Healthcare
Mid-Atlantic
9700 Patuxent Woods Drive
Columbia, MD 21046

MASSACHUSETTS

Patricia Fraser
Brigham and Woman's Hospital
75 St. Francis Street
Boston, MA 02115-6195

Robert P. Sundel
Children's Hospital—Department of Immunology
300 Longwood Avenue
Boston, MA 02146

Daniel B. Magilavy
Biogen
14 Cambridge Center
Cambridge, MA 02142

Laurie C. Miller
Pediatrics
New England Medical Center
750 Washington Box 67
Boston MA 02111

Jane Schaller, M.D.
Tufts University School of Medicine
171 Harrison Avenue
Boston, MA 02111

John L. Sullivan, M.D.
Immunology/Rheumatology
University of Massachusetts Medical School
55 Lake Avenue N.
Worcester, MA 01605-2397

Lori Tucker, M.D.
Floating Hospital
750 Washington Street
Box 286
Boston, MA 02111

MICHIGAN

Barbara S. Adams
University of Michigan
D3216 MPB, 1500 E. Med Ctr Dr
Ann Arbor, MI 48109-0718

Hiliary Haftel
University of Michigan
D3216 MPB, 1500 E. Med Ctr Dr
Ann Arbor, MI 48109-0718

James M. Jarvis, M.D.
Children's Hospital of Michigan
3901 Beaubien
Detroit, MI 48201

Ellen Moore, M.D.
Children's Hospital of Michigan
3901 Beaubien
Detroit, MI 48201

Carol Ragsdale, M.D.
University of Michigan, Department of Pediatrics
D3211 MPB
Ann Arbor, MI 48109-0010

Donita Sullivan, M.D.
Department of Pediatrics
University of Michigan Hospital
D3215 MPB
Ann Arbor, MI 48109

MINNESOTA

George Leighton Allen, M.D.
Mayo Clinic
200 First Street, S.W.
Rochester, MN 55905

Thomas G. Mason, II
Division of Rheumatology
Mayo Clinic Rochester
200 First Street, S.W.
Rochester, MN 55901

Audrey M. Nelson, M.D.
Mayo Clinic
200 First Street, S.W.
Rochester, MN 55905

Richard K. Vehe
University of Minnesota Hospital
Box 817 420 Delaware Street, S.E.
Minneapolis, MN 55455-0392

Joyce K. Warshawsky, M.D.
Minneapolis Children's Medical Center
2545 Chicago Avenue S., Suite 201
Minneapolis, MN 55404

MISSOURI

James T. Cassidy, M.D.
Department of Child Health
One Hospital Drive
Columbia, MO 65212

Jonathan Gitlin
Dept. of Pediatrics
Washington University
One Children's Place
St. Louis, MO 63110

Katherine L. Madson
Rheumatology Center
The Children's Mercy Hospital
2401 Gilham Road
Kansas City, MO 64108

Terry L. Moore, M.D.
St. Louis University—Rheumatology
1402 S. Grand Boulevard
St. Louis, MO 63104

Peri H. Pepmueller
St. Louis University Medical School
Department of Internal Medicine
1402 S. Grand
St. Louis, MO 63104

Catherine S. Tripp
Dept. of Pediatrics
Washington University
One Children's Place
St. Louis, MO 63110

MONTANA

Peggy Schlesinger, M.D.
515 W. Front Street
Missoula, MT 59802

NEBRASKA

Russell Hopp, D.O.
Creighton University Medical Center
Department of Pediatrics
601 N. 30th Street
Omaha, NE 68131

NEW JERSEY

Michael C. Knee, M.D.
Chief of Pediatric Rheumatology
Children's Hospital of New Jersey
15 S. 9th Street
Newark, NJ 07107

NEW YORK

John Baum, M.D.
Monroe Community Hospital
University of Rochester
435 E. Henrietta Road
Rochester, NY 14603

Joan G. Calkins
Western NY Pediatrics
3675 Southwestern Blvd.
Orchard Park, NY 14127

Chun P. Chao
New York Medical College
Munger Pavilion
Valhalla, NY 10595

Andrew Eichenfield, M.D.
Division of Pediatric Rheumatology
Mt. Sinai Medical Center
One Gustave Levy Place
New York, NY 11029-6574

Patricia L Haber
Albert Einstein College of Medicine
1500 Astor Avenue
Bronx, NY 10469

Kathleen A. Haines
Hospital for Joint Diseases
301 East 17th Street, Room 1410
New York, NY 10003

Norman Illowite, M.D.
Immuno/Rheumatology Division
Schneider Children's Hospital of LIJ
Hillside Medical Center
New Hyde Park, NY 11042

Jerry C. Jacobs, M.D.
Columbia University College of Physicians and Surgeons
Rheumatology Department
4621 Waldo Avenue
Riverdale, NY 10471

Thomas Lehman, M.D.
Chief, Division of Pediatric Rheumatology
Hospital for Special Surgery
535 E. 70th Street
New York, NY 10021

Peter R. Logalbo
Schneider Children's Hospital
New Hyde Park, NY 11042

Kathleen M. O'Neil, M.D.
Children's Hospital of Buffalo
219 Bryant Street
Buffalo, NY 14222

NORTH CAROLINA

Theresa Sue Bratton, M.D.
1021 E. Wendover Avenue, Suite 302
Greensboro, NC 27465

Patricia S. Gerber, M.D.
Southeast Allergy Association, PA
2321 Delaney
Wilmington, NC 28403

Deborah W. Kredich, M.D.
Department of Pediatrics
Duke University Medical School
Box 3100, Duke Hospital
Durham, NC 27710

Nick Patrone, M.D.
Boice Willis Clinic
901 N Winstead Ave, Ste 500
Rocky Mountain, NC 27804

Ann M. Reed
University of North Carolina-Chapel Hill
509 Burnett Womack, CB7280
Chapel Hill, NC 27599

Laura E. Schanberg, M.D.
Department of Pediatrics
Duke Medical Center
Box 31204
Durham, NC 27710

Leonard D. Stein
University of North Carolina—Chapel Hill
509 Burnett Womack, CB7220
Chapel Hill, NC 27599

Dorothy W. Wortman
East Carolina School of Medicine
3E-142 Brody Med Science Bldg.
Greenville, NC 27858-4354

OHIO

Jack C. Bass, M.D.
3230 Northwest Boulevard
Columbus, OH 43221

Robert A. Colbert
Children's Hospital Medical Medical Center
Elland & Bethesda Pavillion 2-129
Cincinnati, OH 45229

Jaime Deinocencio
Children's Hospital Medical Medical Center
Elland & Bethesda Pavillion 2-129
Cincinnati, OH 45229

Chris Gabriel, M.D.
2005 Washington Circle
Cincinnati, OH 45212

David Glass, M.D.
Children's Hospital Medical Center
Elland and Bethesda Avenues
Cincinnati, OH 45229-2899

Raphael Hirsch
Children's Hospital Medical Medical Center
Elland & Bethesda Pavillion 2-129
Cincinnati, OH 45229

Joseph Levinson, M.D.
Children's Hospital Medical Center
Division of Rheumatology
Pavilion Building, 1-129
Elland and Bethesda Avenues
Cincinnati, OH 45229

Daniel J. Lovell, M.D., M.P.H.
Children's Hospital Medical Center
Division of Rheumatology
Pavilion Building 1-129
Elland and Bethesda Avenues
Cincinnati, OH 45229

Arthur Newman, M.D.
Rainbow Babies & Children's Hospital
2101 Adelbert Road
Cleveland, OH 44106

Murray Passo, M.D.
Division of Rheumatology
Children's Hospital Medical Center
Pavilion Building 1-129
Cincinnati, OH 45229

Robert M. Rennebohm, M.D.
Arthritis Center
Children's Hospital
700 Children's Drive
Columbus, OH 43205

Steven Shapiro, M.D.
1611 S. Green Road
S. Euclid, OH 44121

Bernhard H. Singsen
The Cleveland Clinic
9500 Euclid
Cleveland, OH 44195

OREGON

Michael S. Borzy, M.D.
Department of Pediatrics
Oregon Health Sciences University
Portland, OR 97201

PENNSYLVANIA

Carolyn H. Anderson, M.D.
100 Delafield Road, Suite 303
Pittsburgh, PA 15255

Balu H. Athreya, M.D.
Children's Seashore House
3405 Civic Center Boulevard
Philadelphia, PA 19104

Donald P. Goldsmith
St. Christopher Hospital for Children
Erie Ave at Front St.
Philadelphia, PA 19134-1095

Susan Hoch
Hahnemann University
245 N. 15th St
Philadelphia, PA 19102

Gregory Keenan
Children's Seashore House
Children's Hospital of Philadelphia
One Civic Center Blvd.
Philadelphia, PA 19104

Aldo V. Londino, M.D.
Director, Arthritis Center
Children's Hospital Pittsburgh
One Children's Place
3705 Fifth Avenue at DeSoto Street
Pittsburgh, PA 15213-3417

Elizabeth Mellins
Children's Seashore House
Children's Hospital of Philadelphia
One Civic Center Blvd.
Philadelphia, PA 19104

Barbara E. Ostrov
Hershey Medical Center
PO Box 850
Hershey, PA 17033

James L. Perruquet, M.D.
Department of Rheumatology
Geisenger Medical Center
N. Academy Drive
Danville, PA 17822

Kathleen Sullivan
Children's Seashore House
Children's Hospital of Philadelphia
One Civic Center Blvd.
Philadelphia, PA 19104

Dennis Torretti, M.D.
Department of Rheumatology
Geisinger Medical Center
Danville, PA 17822

TENNESSEE

Aram S. Hanissian, M.D.
Baptist Memorial Hospital East
2027 Walnut Grove Road
Memphis, TN 38119

J. Kenneth Herd
James H. Quillen
PO Box 70578
Johnson City, TN 37614

Gloria C. Higgins, M.D.
University of Tennessee
Special Research
956 Court Avenue, Room B310
Memphis, TN 38160

Donna Hummel
Vanderbilt University
Medical Center North D3237
Nashville, TN 37232-2580

Alexander Lawton
Vanderbilt University
Medical Center North D3237
Nashville, TN 37232-2580

Linda K. Myers, M.D.
Department of Pediatrics
University of Tennessee Health Sciences Center
956 Court Avenue, B310
Memphis, TN 38163

TEXAS

Norma Battles, M.D.
6959 Arapaho, Suite 523
Dallas, TX 75240

Chester W. Fink, M.D.
Department of Pediatrics
University of Texas Health Sciences Center at Dallas
Southwestern Medical School
Dallas, TX 75235

Linda Gorin, M.D.
2600 Gessner, #218
Houston, TX 77080

Barry Myones
Texas Children's Hospital
6621 Fannin Street
Houston, TX 77030

Maria D. Perez, M.D.
Pediatric Rheumatology
Texas Children's Hospital
6608 Fannin Street, Suite 1
Houston, TX 77030

Marilynn Punaro, M.D.
3965 Cedarbrush Drive
Dallas, TX 75229

Amy Star
Tyler Pediatric Clinic
612 S. Fleishel
Tyler, TX 75701-2012

Robert W. Warren, M.D., Ph.D.
Department of Pediatrics
Baylor College of Medicine
One Baylor Plaza
Houston, TX 77030

Andrew Wilking, M.D.
Texas Children's Hospital
6608 Fannin Street
Houston, TX 77030

UTAH

John Bohnsack
Dept. of Pediatrics
University of Utah Medical Center
50 North Medical Drive
Salt Lake City, UT 84132

W. Patrick Knibbe, M.D.
Adult and Pediatric Rheumatology
324 Tenth Avenue, Suite 250
Salt Lake City, UT 84103

VIRGINIA

Lenore M. Buckley
Department of Pediatrics
Medical College of Virginia
MCV Station Box 102
Richmond, VA 23298

Christos Gabriel, M.D.
Division of Rheumatology
Children's Hospital King's Daughters
601 Children's Lane
Norfolk, VA 23507

Harry L. Gewanter, M.D.
Children's Hospital
2924 Brook Road
Richmond, VA 23220

Anne-Marie A. Irani, M.D.
Medical College of Virginia
MCU Station Box 225
Richmond, VA 23298

Richard W. Kesler, M.D.
Department of Pediatrics
University of Virginia Medical Center
Charlottesville, VA 22908

Paul Rochmis, M.D.
3027 Javier Road
Fairfax, VA 22031

Frank T. Saulsbury, M.D.
University of Virginia Medical Center
Department of Pediatrics
Box 386
Charlottesville, VA 22908

WASHINGTON

Barbara Nepom, M.D.
Virginia Mason Research Center
1000 Seneca
Seattle, WA 98101

David D. Sherry, M.D.
Division of Rheumatology
Children's Hospital & Medical Center
4800 Sand Point Way, N.E.
Seattle, WA 98105

Carol A. Wallace, M.D.
Division of Rheumatology
Children's Hospital & Medical Center
4800 Sand Point Way, N.E.
Seattle, WA 98105

Ralph J. Wedgwood, M.D.
Department of Rheumatology
Children's Orthopedic Hospital
P. O. Box C5371
Seattle, WA 98105

WISCONSIN

Edward B. Blau, M.D.
Marshfield Clinic
100 N. Oak
Marshfield, WI 54449

James J. Nocton
Medical College of Wisconsin
9000 W. Wisconsin Ave
Milwaukee, WI 53226

Judy Olsen, M.D.
8701 Watertown Plank Road
Milwaukee, WI 53226

PUERTO RICO

Yvonne L. Arroyo, M.D.
Tarragona #510
Urb. Matienzo Cintron
Puerto Rico, 00923

CANADA

James Boone, M.D.
800 Commissioners Road, East
London, Ontario
Canada N6A 4G5

Peter Dent, M.D.
McMaster University
Department of Pediatrics
1200 Main Street West
Hamilton, Ontario
Canada L8N 3Z5

Janet E. Ellsworth, M.D.
University of Alberta Medical Center
2C3.31 Walter Mackenzie Center
Edmonton, Alberta
Canada T6G 2B7

Katherine R. Gross, M.D.
19764 20th Avenue RR1
Langley, British Columbia
Canada V3A 4P4

Robert Hill, M.D.
B.C.'s Children's Hospital
4480 Oak Street
Vancouver, British Columbia
Canada V6H 3V4

Ronald N. Laxer, MDCM FRCP
181 Willowbrook Road
Thornhill, Ontario
Canada L3T 5L5

Peter Malleson, M.D.
4077 W. 34th Avenue
Vancouver, British Columbia
Canada V6N 2L6

Kiem Oen, M.D.
Pediatrics RR149 Rehabilitation Center
800 Sherbrook Street
Winnipeg, Manitoba
Canada R3A 1M4

Ross Petty, M.D., Ph.D.
Department of Pediatrics
University of British Columbia
Research Center Room 217
950 W. 28th Avenue
Vancouver, British Columbia
Canada V5Z 4H4

Alan M. Rosenberg, M.D.
Department of Pediatrics
University Hospital
University of Saskatchewan
Saskatoon, Saskatchewan
Canada S7N 0X0

Anthony Russell, FRCP
University of Alberta
9-112 Clinical Science
Edmonton, Alberta
Canada T6G 2G3

Abraham D. Shore, M.D.
Wellesley Hospital - Rheumatology
160 Wellesley Street E
Toronto, Ontario
Canada

Earl Silverman, M.D.
Hospital for Sick Children
555 University Avenue
Toronto, Ontario
Canada M5G 1X8

MEXICO

R. Burgos-Vargos
Dr. Balmis 148, Colonia
Mexico City, Mexico 06726

Egle Delgado, M.D.
Guerrero 1-B
San Juan del Rio, Qro
Mexico

Manuel Martinez-Lavin, M.D.
Inst. NAC Cardiologia
Periferico Sur y Viaducto
Tlalpan, Mexico City
DF Mexico

Directory of Pediatric
Rheumatology Centers

The following list of centers is undoubtedly incomplete. Check with your physician or local chapter of the Arthritis Foundation to find out the names of others near you.

ARIZONA

University Medical Center
1501 N. Campbell Avenue
Tucson, AZ 85724
(602) 626-6527

ARKANSAS

Arkansas Children's Hospital
UAMS
800 Marshall Street
Little Rock, AR 72202
(501) 370-1401

CALIFORNIA

Cedars-Sinai Medical Center
8700 Beverly Boulevard
Los Angeles, CA 90048
(213) 855-4441

Children's Hospital of Los Angeles
4650 Sunset Boulevard
Los Angeles, CA 90048
(213) 669-2119

UCLA Department of Pediatrics
Center for Health Sciences
Los Angeles, CA 90024
(213) 825-6481

Children's Hospital of Orange County
455 S. Main Street
Orange, CA 92668
(714) 532-8617

Children's Hospital of Stanford
520 Sand Hill Road
Palo Alto, CA 94304
(415) 327-4800

University of California, San Francisco
Department of Pediatrics
Room M-679
San Francisco, CA 94143
(415) 476-1736

COLORADO

Rocky Mountain Juvenile Arthritis Center
National Jewish Hospital
1400 Jackson Street
Denver, CO 80206
(303) 398-1378

CONNECTICUT

Newington Children's Hospital
181 E. Cedar Street
Newington, CT 06111
(203) 667-5591

Department of Pediatrics
Yale School of Medicine
333 Cedar Street
New Haven, CT 06510-3289

DELAWARE

Alfred I. Dupont Institute
1600 Rockland Road
Wilmington, DE 19899
(302) 651-5970

DISTRICT OF COLUMBIA

Children's National Medical Center
111 Michigan Avenue, N.W
Washington, DC 20010-2970
(202) 745-548

Georgetown University
Division of Rheumatology
3800 Reservoir Road, N.W.
Washington, DC 20007
(202) 687-8233

Walter Reed Army Medical Center
Department of Rheumatology
Washington, DC 20307-5001
(202) 576-1735

FLORIDA

Miami Children's Hospital
3200 S.W. 60 Court, Suite 205
Miami, FL 33155
(305) 663-8505

University of South Florida,
School of Medicine,
13000 Bruce Downs Blvd.
Tampa, Florida 33612

GEORGIA

Atlanta Regional Pediatric Rheumatology Center
1740 Century Circle, N.E., Suite 14
Atlanta, GA 30034
(404) 634-7556

HAWAII

Pediatric Arthritis Center of Hawaii
1319 Punahou Street, Suite 734
Honolulu, HI 96826
(808) 945-7725

Tripler Army Medical Center
Department of Pediatrics
Honolulu, HI 96859-5000
(808) 433-6474

ILLINOIS

La Rabida Children's Hospital & Research Center
E. 65th Street at Lake Michigan
Chicago, IL 60649
(312) 363-6700

The Children's Memorial Hospital
Pediatric Arthritis Center
2300 Children's Plaza
Chicago, IL 60614
(312) 820-4360

University of Illinois at Chicago
Pediatric Rheumatology Clinic
840 S. Wood Street
Chicago, IL 60612
(312) 996-6714

INDIANA

Riley Hospital for Children
702 Barnhill Drive
Indianapolis, IN 46223
(317) 274-2172

KANSAS

University of Kansas Medical Center
39th & Rainbow
Kansas City, KS 66103
(913) 588-6325

KENTUCKY

University of Kentucky Medical Center
800 Rose Street
Lexington, KY 40536-0084
(606) 233-6799

Dept. of Pediatrics
University of Louisville
School of Medicine
Louisville, KY 40292

LOUISIANA

Children's Hospital
200 Henry Clay Avenue
New Orleans, LA 70118
(504) 899-9511

MARYLAND

The Johns Hopkins Hospital
600 N. Wolfe Street
Baltimore, MD 21205
(301) 955-6145

Bethesda Naval Hospital
4301 Jones Bridge Road
Bethesda, MD 20814-5011
(301) 295-4900

MASSACHUSETTS

Brigham and Women's Hospital
 Juvenile & Adolescent Rheumatology Program
75 Francis Street
Boston, MA 02115
(617) 732-5323

Children's Hospital
Rheumatology Program
300 Longwood Avenue
Boston, MA 02115-5747
(617) 735-6117

Massachusetts General Hospital
WACC 7
15 Parkman Street, Suite 615
Boston, MA 02114
(617) 726-7938

The Floating Hospital for Infants & Children
Pediatric Rheumatology Division
750 Washington Street
Boston, MA 02111
(617) 956-5071

University of Massachusetts Medical Center
55 Lake Avenue, North
Worcester, MA 01655
(508) 856-3947

MICHIGAN

University of Michigan Medical Center
1500 E. Medical Center Drive
Ann Arbor, MI 48108-0718
(313) 764-2224

Children's Hospital of Michigan
3901 Beaubien
Detroit, MI 48201
(313) 745-5566

MSU Clinical Center for Child Health
Division of Pediatrics
Michigan State University
Clinical Center Service Road
East Lansing, MI 48824
(517) 353-3002

MINNESOTA

University of Minnesota
420 Delaware Street
Minneapolis, MN 55455
(612) 624-5146

Mayo Clinic
200 First Avenue, S.W.
Rochester, MN 55905
(507) 284-2973

Gillette Children's Hospital
200 East University
St. Paul, MN 55101
(612) 229-3893

MISSOURI

University of Missouri–Columbia
Division of Pediatric Rheumatology
One Hospital Drive
Columbia, MO 65212
(314) 882-3996

Children's Mercy Hospital
24th at Gillham Road
Kansas City, MO 64108
(816) 234-3000

St. Louis University Medical Center
1402 S. Grand Boulevard
St. Louis, MO 63104
(314) 577-8467

MONTANA

Western Montana Clinic
515 W. Front Street
Missoula, MT 59802
(406) 721-5600

NEBRASKA

Creighton University
Department of Pediatrics
601 N. 30th Street
Omaha, NE 68131
(402) 280-4580

NEW JERSEY

Robert Wood Johnson Medical School
Children's Arthritis Program
One Robert Wood Johnson Place, CN19
New Brunswick, NJ 08903-0019
(201) 937-7702

St. Joseph's Hospital & Medical Center
Pediatric Subspecialties
703 Main Street
Paterson, NJ 07503
(201) 977-2401

NEW YORK

Children's Hospital of Buffalo
219 Bryant Street
Buffalo, NY 14222
(716) 878-7105

Schneider Children's Hospital
Pediatric Rheumatology
LIJ Medical Center, Room 235
New Hyde Park, NY 11042
(718) 470-3306

Columbia University College of Physicians & Surgeons
Babies Hospital
New York, NY 10032
(212) 305-8585

Hospital for Joint Diseases
301 E. 17th Street
New York, NY 10003
(212) 598-6516

Hospital for Special Surgery
535 E. 70th Street
New York, NY 10021
(212) 606-1151

Mount Sinai School of Medicine
1 Gustave L. Levy Place
New York, NY 10029-6574
(212) 241-6933

New York Hospital/Cornell Medical Center
525 E. 68th Street
New York, NY 10021
(212) 606-1151

NORTH CAROLINA

Duke/University of North Carolina Pediatric Rheumatology Center
Box 3212 Duke Hospital
Durham, NC 27710
(919) 684-6575

East Carolina School of Medicine
3516 Brody
Greenville, NC 27834
(919) 551-2533

OHIO

Children's Hospital Medical Center
Elland and Bethesda Avenues
Cincinnati, OH 45229-2899
(513) 559-4676

Rainbow Babies and Children's Hospital
2103 Adelbert Road
Cleveland, OH 44106
(216) 844-4795

Children's Hospital Arthritis Center
700 Children's Drive
Columbus, OH 43205
(614) 461-2251

OKLAHOMA

Oklahoma Arthritis Care Center
701 N.E. 10th Street
Oklahoma City, OK 73104
(405) 271-2273

PENNSYLVANIA

Children's Hospital of Pittsburgh
Pediatric Rheumatology Center
125 de Soto Street
Pittsburgh, PA 15213
(412) 692-7486

Children's Seashore House
Children's Hospital of Philadelphia
3400 Civic Center Boulevard
Philadelphia, PA 19104
(215) 590-2428

Section of Rheumatology
St. Christopher's Hospital for Children
Erie Ave. at Front St.
Philadelphia, PA 19134-1095

Geisinger Medical Center
North Academy Ave.
Danville, PA 17821

Hershey Medical Center
PO Box 850
Hershey, PA 17033

Mercy Children's Medical Center
1400 Locust Street
Pittsburgh, PA 15219
(412) 232-7288

TENNESSEE

Le Bonheur Hospital
University of Tennessee–Memphis
848 Adams Street
Memphis, TN 38103
(901) 522-3224

TEXAS

University of Texas Southwestern Medical Center
Division of Pediatric Rheumatology
5323 Harry Hines Boulevard
Dallas, TX 75235
(214) 688-3388

Pediatric Rheumatology Center
UTHSC, Department of Pediatrics
7703 Floyd Curl Drive
San Antonio, TX 78284
(512) 567-5304

Texas Children's Hospital
Regional Pediatric Rheumatology Center
6621 Fannin
Houston, TX 77030
(713) 798-2929

Children's Hospital of Austin
Rheumatology Program
601 E. 15th Street
Austin, TX 78701
(512) 480-1828

Pediatric Rheumatology Clinic
Border Children's Health Center
Providence Memorial Hospital
2001 N. Oregon Street
El Paso, TX 79902
(915) 532-1156

UTAH

University of Utah Medical School
50 North Medical Drive
Salt Lake City, UT 84102
(801) 581-5873

VIRGINIA

Children's Hospital
2924 Brook Road
Richmond, VA 23220
(804) 321-7474

Fairfax Hospital for Children
3299 Woodburn Road
Annadale, VA 22003

Medical College of Virginia
P.O. Box 225
11th and Marshall Streets
Richmond, VA 23298
(804) 786-9620

University of Virginia Children's Medical Center
Department of Pediatrics
Box 386
Charlottesville, VA 22908
(804) 924-2357

WASHINGTON

Children's Hospital & Medical Center
4800 Sand Point Way, N.E
Seattle, WA 98105
(206) 526-2057

WISCONSIN

Medical College of Wisconsin
Children's Hospital of Wisconsin
9000 W. Wisconsin
P.O. Box 1997
Milwaukee, WI 53201
(414) 266-2850

CANADA

University of Alberta Hospital
8440 112th Street
Edmonton, Alberta T6G 2R7
Canada
(403) 492-6631
British Columbia's Children's Hospital
4480 Oak Street
Vancouver, British Columbia V6H 3V4
Canada
(604) 879-7511

Children's Hospital
RR149 - 800 Sherbrook Street
Winnipeg, Manitoba R3A 1M4
Canada
(204) 787-2020

Children's Hospital at Chedoke McMaster
1200 Main Street, West
Hamilton, Ontario N6C 2V5
Canada
(416) 521-2100

Children's Hospital of Western Ontario
800 Commissioner's Road, East
London, Ontario N6V 2V5
Canada
(519) 685-8130

The Hospital for Sick Children
555 University Avenue
Toronto, Ontario M5G 1X8
Canada
(416) 598-6117

Hôpital Ste-Justine
3175 Ch. Cote Ste-Catherine
Montreal, Quebec 83T 1C5
Canada
(514) 345-4713

Montreal Children's Hospital
2300 Tupper Street, Room A-218
Montreal, Quebec H3H 1P3
Canada
(514) 934-4400

University Hospital
Department of Pediatrics
Saskatoon, Saskatchewan S7N 0X0
Canada
(306) 966-8112

Appendix C

Publications

AJAO RESOURCE CATALOGUE 1995

This excellent catalogue is a must publication for parents, children, and young adults. The resource contains specific print materials prepared by the American Juvenile Arthritis Organization, proceedings from the annual conferences of the AJAO, general print materials for parents, young adults, health professionals, children, teens, and siblings, newsletters, videocassette programs, and sound/slide programs. 52 pages.

Order: Arthritis Foundation
          1314 Spring Street, N.W.
          Atlanta, Georgia 30309

Price: One copy free.

Arthritis in Children and La Artritis Infanojuvenil
Arthritis Foundation - revised, 1993

A medical information booklet about JRA written for parents or other adults. Includes details about the different forms of JRA, medications, therapies, and coping issues. (Also available in Spanish.)

Order: Your local Arthritis Foundation Chapter.

Price: Free (single copy)

Fathers of Children with Special Needs: New Horizons

May, James, 1990

This text deals with the concerns of fathers of children with special needs, often quite different from those of mothers. It discusses issues of service delivery and how professionals can encourage the involvement of fathers in the care of their children. It outlines the development of father support groups, as well as resources for fathers and their families.

Order: ACCH
7910 Woodmont Avenue, Suite 300
Bethesda, MD 20814
(301) 654-6549

Price: $3.95, 10 copies or more $3.50 each.

When Your Student Has Arthritis: A Guide for Teachers

Arthritis Foundation - revised, 1989

A medical information booklet written for teachers or other adults who know children with arthritis. The pamphlet describes different forms of JRA, how arthritis might affect the child at school, and how to help the child work around these problems. (Parents have found this booklet very helpful as a basic introduction to help teachers understand arthritis-related problems.)

Order: Your local Arthritis Foundation Chapter or
Arthritis Foundation - Patient Services Department
1314 Spring Street, N.W.
Atlanta, GA 30309
(404) 872-7100

Price: Free - single copy

Recreational and Physical Activity for the Child with Juvenile Arthritis: A Guide for Teachers

Nicholson, C., Del Vecchio, J. A., Rosenberg, M., Washington, D.C., April 1986

A guide for teachers, recommending that children with arthritis be encouraged to participate in individual and group physical activities. Continued movement helps prevent loss of range of motion, strength, and endurance. When joints are swollen and painful, a modified physical education program is necessary. Specific methods of performing different activities are described to replace stressful ones. There is a list of recommended indoor and outdoor activities, and a list of activities to be avoided. The guide is reprinted at the end of Appendix C.

Order: Comprehensive Pediatric Rheumatology Center
         Children's Hospital National Medical Center
         111 Michigan Avenue, N.W.
         Washington, DC 20010
         (202) 745-3203

Price: Free

You, Your Child and Arthritis

Shore, Dr. Abraham; Boone, Dr. James

This booklet provides an overview of JRA, including sections of diagnosis, special problems, special types, treatment, the family, independence, school, and adolescence.

Order: Arthritis Society National Office
         920 Yonge Street, Suite 420
         Toronto, M4W 3J7
         Canada

Price: Free

Why Exercise?

Romick, B. J., 1984

This illustrated booklet can be used to help children with JRA understand the need to exercise. It is designed to help them understand how their joints work, what happens inside their joints when they have arthritis, why arthritis makes joints lose motion, and how exercise helps their joints. Ideas are included to help the child remember to exercise. A short quiz follows each section.

Order: Special Treatment Center for Juvenile Arthritis
         Children's Hospital Medical Center
         Elland and Bethesda Avenues
         Cincinnati, OH 45229

Price: $2 each

A Difference in the Family: Living with a Disabled Child

Featherstone, Helen, 1980

Written by a mother of a child with disabilities, this book focuses on how families cope with the disability, the feelings of fear, anger, guilt, and loneliness. It includes interviews with parents and professionals. It discusses marital stress and sibling relationships.

Order: Penguin Books, Ltd.
           40 W. 23rd Street
           New York, NY 10010
Price: $6.95

Arthritis in Children: Resources for Children, Parents, and Teachers

National Institute for Arthritis and Musculoskeletal and Skin Diseases (NIAMS) Information Clearing House - 1987

An annotated bibliography of 100 print and audio-visual materials about arthritis in children.

Order: NIAMS Information Clearinghouse
           P.O. Box AMS
           Bethesda, MD 20892
           (301) 468-3235
Price: $3

Educational Rights for Children with Arthritis: A Manual for Parents

Wetherbee, Linda L., M.S., Neil, Amy J., M.S., 1989

The purpose of this manual is to educate parents of children with rheumatic diseases about obtaining services and accommodations for their children in school. Chapters include questions and exercises to help the reader understand concepts and apply them to their own situation. Additional information from other sources is included in some chapter appendixes. This manual was developed through the collaborative efforts of parents, health professionals, and experts in the fields of special education and instructional design, with a grant from the Ronald McDonald Children's Charities. (This is truly an outstanding aid for all parents with school-age children!)

Order: American Juvenile Arthritis Organization
Arthritis Foundation
1314 Spring Street, N.W.
Atlanta, GA 30309

Price: $6

We Can: A Guide for Parents of Children with Arthritis

Arthritis Foundation, 1990

This 82-page manual suggests practical ways to help make life with arthritis easier. It offers specific tips for day-to-day living, as well as points to keep in mind as parents raise their children. (We highly recommend this manual!)

Order: Patient Services Department
Arthritis Foundation
1314 Spring Street, N.W.
Atlanta, GA 30309

Price: $1.50

AJAO Newsletter

Arthritis Foundation

A quarterly publication of the American Juvenile Arthritis Organization (AJAO), providing current information about issues affecting children with rheumatic diseases. Standard features include *Ask the (Health Professional)*, *Resources!*, *Government Affairs News*, *Executive Committee News*, *Readers' Exchange*, *AJAO in the Community*, and *For Kids Only* (special insert for children).

Order: American Juvenile Arthritis Organization
1314 Spring Street, N.W.
Atlanta, GA 30309
(404) 872-7100

Price: Free with $10 membership in AJAO

JRA and Me

Rocky Mountain Juvenile Arthritis Center and the Arthritis Foundation, 1988

A workbook for school-age children with JRA, including a variety of educational games, puzzles, and worksheets to teach children about their illness and how to take care of themselves.

Order: Your local Arthritis Foundation Chapter

Price: $4.50 (plus postage and handling in some areas).

(I would recommend all of the materials produced at the Center in Hawaii by Dr. Raquel Hicks' team. Their bright, upbeat attitude is very appealing to children.)

Exercise With Kela

Pediatric Arthritis Center of Hawaii, 1985

This pamphlet/flipchart depicts exercise routines with simple instructions: "stand up," "sit down," "lie down," followed by a full exercise routine in that position. Neck, shoulder, elbow, wrist, hand, hip, knee, ankle, and toe exercises are demonstrated. The character Kela works out with "weights" using a stuffed teddy bear or a rubber duck. Aimed at ages two to six, although enjoyable for older children, too.

Order: Kapiolani Medical Center for Women and Children
           Learning Resource Center
           1319 Punahou Street
           Suite 756
           Honolulu, HI 96826

Price: $10.40

Getting Through the Day with Kela

Pediatric Center of Hawaii, 1985

This book addresses the activities of daily living in a fashion that is appealing to young children. Principles of joint protection and energy conservation are depicted in a creative manner utilizing the Kela character. Kela goes through a whole day of activities and shows the children the right way and wrong way of doing things. She is shown brushing teeth, combing hair, holding a cup, holding a pencil, carrying a school bag, putting on clothes and shoes, and so on. On the left side of each page a "Do" column is depicted; on the right, a "Don't" is shown. This pamphlet/flipchart is geared to the young preschool or school-age child four to eight years old.

Order: Kapiolani Medical Center for Women and Children
Learning Resource Center
1319 Punahou Street
Suite 756
Honolulu, HI 96826

Price: $5

Games Kela Plays

Pediatric Center of Hawaii, 1985

The Kela character is again depicted here, showing the games recommended for the young JRA child. We often tell children what they shouldn't do. This pamphlet/flipchart emphasizes what they *can* do and what is actually recommended. Games like Frisbee throwing, passing the ball, turning a rope, badminton, riding a tricycle, and playing with Play-Doh are depicted. Recommended for children four to eight years old, but can be appreciated by somewhat older children.

Order: Kapiolani Medical Center for Women and Children
Learning Resource Center
1319 Punahou Street
Suite 756
Honolulu, HI 96826

Let's Learn About JRA with Kela

Pediatric Arthritis Center of Hawaii, 1985

A pamphlet/flipchart discusses disease activity, medicines, exercise, joint protection, and body position.

Order: Kapiolani Medical Center for Women and Children
Learning Resource Center
1319 Punahou Street
Suite 756
Honolulu, HI 96826

Price: $25

Understanding Juvenile Rheumatoid Arthritis

Arthritis Foundation, 1988

A manual for health professionals to use in teaching children with JRA and their families about disease management and self-care. Each of the 14 topics addressed provides an associated teaching plan. The manual also contains chapters on developmental issues and the teaching/learning process. The manual comes with the *JRA Educational Resources Packet,* which contains samples of related educational materials.

Order: Your local Arthritis Foundation Chapter

Price: $50 plus postage and handling

Jodie's Journey

Thiele, Colin, 1988

An authentic case history of a girl with juvenile arthritis whose spirit refuses to be broken even when it appears her dream of being a champion horseback rider can't come true. Neither the disease itself nor the rudeness, ignorance, and misunderstanding of others can stop Jodie on the personal journey she must take.

Order: Harper Collins Publishers
          Keystone Industrial Park
          Scranton, PA 18512
          (800) 242-7737

Price: $13.95

Diet and Nutrition: Facts to Consider

Arthritis Foundation

This pamphlet discusses basic nutrition, vitamins, and other questions related to arthritis and diet.

Order: Your local Arthritis Foundation Chapter

Price: Free

Nutrition and Your Health: Dietary Guidelines for Americans

U.S. Department of Agriculture, U.S. Department of Health and Human Services, 1985

This pamphlet is a guide to foods we need for good health, foods we should avoid for good health, desirable weight ranges, calories expended in different activities, and so forth.

Order: Human Nutrition Information Service
          U.S. Department of Agriculture
          Room 325A, Federal Building
          Hyattsville, MD 20782
          (Home and Garden Bulletin No. 232)

A Food Guide for the First Five Years

Educational Department, National Live Stock & Meat Board, 1987

This terrific 17-page pamphlet outlines the dietary needs of children in their most formative stages. Their needs are very different from those of an adult. This is very helpful!

Order: Education Department
          National Live Stock & Meat Board
          444 N. Michigan Avenue
          Chicago, IL 60611

Guide to Good Eating

National Dairy Council, 1989

This is a colorful chart showing the different food groups and healthful recommendations for your diet. It is also available in Spanish.

Order: National Dairy Council
          Rosemond, IL 60018-4233

Videocassette Programs

Given how difficult it can be to get to meetings, especially for families living in rural areas, these videotapes are an invaluable learning aid. We highly recommend each of these tapes.

Aquanastics

Vostrejs, Mary Diane, RPT, 1986. 1¾" videocassette (5 min.)

This videotape is designed to describe a water program for children with JRA. It is intended as background information for other therapists to use to begin similar programs.

Order: Mary Diane Vostrejs
        National Jewish Center for Immunology and Respiratory
            Medicine, Department of Pediatrics
        9 Goodman
        1400 Jackson Street
        Denver, CO 80206

Price: For loan only (free)

Age-Related Physical Therapy Programs

Jasso, M., 1984, ½" VHS videocassette (15 min.)

Shows how a physical therapy regime can fit into a child's routine without having it impede her daily life. It illustrates different methods for handling problems that may occur during a typical school day and ways to deal with pain, stiffness, and limited mobility. It discusses how helpful parents, siblings, teachers, and classmates can also provide needed support.

Order: Arthritis Foundation
        Patient Services Department
        1314 Spring Street, N.W.
        Atlanta, GA 30309
        (404) 872-7100

Price: Free (loan)

Maintaining Children Within the School System: Parent Advocacy Training

Athreya, B., M.D., Donivan, F., Ph.D., 1985, ½" VHS videocassette (33 min.) and discussion leader's guide.

Dr. Balu Athreya outlines how his pediatric rheumatology center works with families and with school systems to keep children with arthritis in school. He emphasizes the need to look for strengths in the child and the importance of building on those strengths, and of planning for growth, not just for illness. He outlines some barriers to remaining in school and discusses practical ways to overcome them. Dr. Donivan describes a workshop which is designed to equip parents with information about their legal rights and also with advocacy skills which will enable them to deal effectively with their child's school system.

Order: American Juvenile Arthritis Organization
         Arthritis Foundation
         1314 Spring Street, N.W.
         Atlanta, GA 30309
         (404) 872-7100

Price: Free (loan)

Childhood Arthritis: A Team Effort

Baumgartner, J., Chamberlain, J., 1983, ¾" or ½" VHS or Beta 1 videocassette (12 min.)

Presents various therapy techniques and behavioral strategies that are used in doing exercises with children with JRA. Eight children, varying in ages from 18 months to 13 years, are depicted. They are shown in therapy, school, and at home. Concerns common to therapists, nurses, teachers, and parents who deal with children with JRA are discussed.

Order: Peggy Dibbern
         National Jewish Hospital
         Old Beaumont Building, Room 204
         3800 E. Colfax Avenue
         Denver, CO 80206
         (303) 398-1378

Price: Free (loan)

Overview of Proceedings from the Annual Conferences of the American Juvenile Arthritis Organization

1989, 1½" VHS videocassette (15min.) plus three discussion guides

The purpose of the AJAO videotape collection is to provide information, education, and support for parents of children with JRA, family members, young adults with arthritis, health professionals, and interested others. The videotapes are useful for individuals unable to attend the annual AJAO conferences, support group meetings, and local AJAO conferences. This program included excerpts from the videotapes, "The Power of Parents" (1988); "Rehabilitation: Moving Toward Independence" (1987); "Young Adult Panel: Let's Identify Issues" (1988).

Order: American Juvenile Arthritis Organization
            Arthritis Foundation
            1314 Spring Street, N.W.
            Atlanta, GA 30309

Price: This collection of tapes is free on loan for two weeks,
            to make copies, or available for purchase at cost of duplication.

Proceedings from the Annual Conference of the American Juvenile Arthritis Organization: Advocacy and Organizational Issues

1984 –1988, 10 ½" VHS videocassettes (312 min.) plus 10 discussion guides

This gives an overview of the structure of the AJAO and theArthritis Foundation and describes ways people can become involved with these organizations. It explains how to obtain services for children within the school and health care systems. Includes "AJAO: Our Children's Future Depends on Your Involvement" (1986, 37 min.); " Dwight Schultz: Actor and National Chairman" (1986, 60 min.); "Maintaining Children Within the School System" (and "Parent Training and Advocacy," 1985, 33 min.); "Objectives of the Arthritis Foundation and Future Goals of the AJAO" (1985, 32 min.); "Organizing a Parent Group" (1985, 30 min.); "Overview of Services to Health-Impaired Children: Past, Present and Future" (1985, 24 min.); "The Power of Parents" (1988, 25 min.); "Special Needs of Chronically Ill Children in the School Setting: Part I (1985, 27 min.) and Part II" (1985, 24 min.).

Order: American Juvenile Arthritis Organization
            Arthritis Foundation
            1314 Spring Street, N.W.
            Atlanta, GA 30309

Price: Same as above

Proceedings from the Annual Conferences of the American Juvenile Arthritis Organization: Family, Psychosocial, and Coping Issues

1984–1988, 15 ½" VHS videocassettes (551 min.) plus 15 discussion guides.

Describes how chronic illness affects the child and family, and describes techniques for coping with chronic illness and maintaining self-esteem. Shows how to have increased optimism and motivation by hearing the personal experiences of others living with these diseases. Includes "Care for the Care-Giver" (1988, 47 min.); "Developing Strategies to Deal with a Long-Term Illness" (1986, 49 min.); "Does Arthritis Cause Temper Tantrums?" (1988, 33 min.); "The Family: Making the Difference" (1988, 49 min.); "Growing Up with Juvenile Arthritis: Perspectives as Adults" (1986, 61 min.); "Growing Up with JRA" (1984, 14 min.); "Helping Your Child Develop Self-Esteem" (1986, 52 min.); "The Impact of Chronic Illness on Families" (1984, 12 min.); "The Impact of Chronic Illness on the Child" (1984, 15 min.); "The Impact of Chronic Illness on the Family" (1987, 47 min.); "Maintaining Self-Esteem in Children and Teenagers" (1984, 28 min.); "Overcoming Disabilities: Our Promise and Potential" (1985, 25 min.); "Panel Discussion: Advice from Parents" (1986, 36 min.); "Siblings of Children with Chronic Illness" (1987, 38 min.); "Young Adult Panel: Let's Identify Issues" (1988, 45 min.).

Order: Same as above

Price: Same as above

Proceedings from the Annual Conference of the American Juvenile Arthritis Organization: Financial Issues

1987, 1 ½" VHS videocassette (33 min.) and discussion guide

This tape describes different types of health insurance coverage and high-risk insurance pools. It shows how to evaluate and purchase health insurance policies. Includes "Family Financial Preparedness."

Order: Same as above

Proceedings from the Annual Conference of the American Juvenile Arthritis Organization: Medical Information

1984–1988, eight ½" VHS videocassettes (281 min.) plus eight discussion guides

Describes specific diseases such as JRA, systemic lupus erythematosus, and the role of medication and nutrition in treatment, and increases confidence in identifying and evaluating alternative treatments. Includes "Anti-Rheumatic Medications" (1984, 18 min.); "Eye Problems in Children with Rheumatic Diseases" (1985, 45 min.); "Information on Juvenile

Arthritis for Newly Diagnosed Families" (1986, 37 min.); "Mixed Connective Tissue Disease (MCTD)" (1986, 41 min.); "Nutrition, Its Role in Arthritis" (1986, 36 min.); "Overview of Rheumatic Diseases: Part I" (1987, 38 min.); "Overview of Rheumatic Diseases: Part II" (1987, 35 min.); "Systemic Lupus Erythematosus" (1988, 31 min.).

Order: Same as above

Proceedings from the Annual Conference of the American Juvenile Arthritis Organization: Therapy and Rehabilitation Issues

1984 –1988, eight ½" VHS videocassettes (235 min.) plus eight discussion guides

These discussions will give the viewer increased confidence when interacting with health professionals about rehabilitation issues. It describes specific ideas for promoting independence in their children and ways to make children's therapy programs creative and fun. Includes "Age-Related Physical Therapy Program" (1984, 21 min.); "Be Care-Full: Body Mechanics" (1988, 18 min.); "Creativity in the Rehabilitation Process" (1987, 36 min.); "JRA: A Team Approach" (1984, 15 min.); "Orthopedic Problems and Joint Replacements in Children with JRA" (1985, 33 min.); "Recreation and Sports for Children with Arthritis" (1986, 26 min.); "Rehabilitation: Moving Toward Independence" (1987, 57 min.).

Order: Same as above

Proceedings from the Annual Conference of the American Juvenile Arthritis Organization: Young Adult Issues

1984–1988, five ½" VHS videocassettes and five discussion guides.

These tapes help to increase confidence in coping with arthritis in social situations, at home, and at work. Also, hearing other adults share their personal experiences growing up with arthritis may increase optimism and motivation. Includes "The Family: Making the Difference" (1988, 49 min.); "Maintaining Self-Esteem in Children and Teenagers" (1984, 28 min.); "Overcoming Disabilities: Our Promise and Potential" (1985, 25 min.); "Vocational Training, Educational and Career Opportunities" (1985, 38 min.); "Young Adult Panel: Let's Identify Issues" (1988, 45 min.).

Order: Same as above

Special Kids, Special Dads: Fathers of Children with Disabilities

May, J., 1989, ½" or ¾" videotape, 23 min.

This unique training film focuses on the emotional needs of fathers and the importance of involving fathers in the care of their children with special needs.

Order: ACCH
7910 Woodmont Avenue, Suite 300
Bethesda, MD 20814
(301) 654-6549

Price: ½" $80 (#7266-1) ¾" $80 (7267-1)

Recreational and Physical Activity for the Child with Juvenile Arthritis:

A Guide for Teachers

Carol Nicholson, R.P.T.

Jo Ann Del Vecchio, O.T.R.

Marcia Rosenberg, R.P.T.

Children's Hospital National Medical Center

Comprehensive Rheumatology Center

Individual and group physical activities are very important for the child with juvenile arthritis because they help to maintain and improve joint mobility, muscle strength, and endurance. When the child is experiencing a "flare-up," one or more of her joints will be warm to touch, swollen, and painful. During this acute stage of disease activity, less strenuous activities are recommended to minimize stress on the involved joints. The child should begin to play more actively after the swelling and pain decrease, and if this does not happen, encouragement from parents, teachers, and therapists is helpful. When the child's arthritis is well controlled with medication, and there is no joint pain and/or swelling, the child should return to a normal level of physical activity. Continued movement is essential to prevent loss of range of motion, strength, and endurance.

The child with JRA should be encouraged to participate in physical education class as much as possible. If many joints are involved, or if the child's joints are very swollen and painful, the child will have limited endurance for exercise and will need frequent rest periods. During times of acute pain and swelling, a modified physical education program should be developed. For example, a lightweight Nerfball or a beachball can be substituted for a volleyball or a basketball to decrease stress on the hands, wrists, elbows, and shoulders. Whiffle ball can be played instead of softball or baseball, and badminton instead of tennis. To protect the hips, knees, and ankles, dance and other movement exercises can be performed on a mat rather than on a hard surface. Physical and occupational therapists are able to assist in developing an exercise program specifically designed for the child's physical needs.

One of the most beneficial activities for the child with arthritis is swimming, as it helps to increase strength and mobility, to improve aerobic conditioning, and to promote socialization. The buoyancy of the water makes it easy to move painful joints. For example, walking is easy in water, even though it may be painful on land. Other positive aquatic experiences are relay games, beachball activities, kicking, and breathing exercises. Basic guidelines for the child when swimming are as follows:

1. Wear warm clothing before and after pool activities to avoid becoming chilled.

2. Swim when well rested, and take time out of each hour for a rest period.

3. Prior to swimming, perform warm-up exercises in the water, including gentle stretching.

4. When a joint is swollen, warm, and painful, exercise gently.

5. If pain increases after swimming, take it a little easier the next time.

Another excellent activity for the child with JRA is pedaling, as it encourages mobility and strengthening for the legs, as well as general conditioning. Pedal toys can be used for small children. If a child is afraid of falling off a bicycle, training wheels and encouragement will help the child learn to ride. Initially, pedaling should be done on level ground, progressing to pedaling uphill. Similarly, paddleboats are also a fun way to increase mobility and strength.

When choosing indoor activities, one must consider how long the child will be sitting or standing, as well as the position of the neck and hands. Prolonged sitting and static positioning of the neck and hands promotes stiffness and soft tissue tightness, and should be avoided. Many activities can be done while the child is lying on her stomach, which is recommended when there is hip and knee involvement. Wrist splints can be worn during play, unless the project is extremely "messy." To encourage reaching, projects such as macrame can be placed on a peg on the wall above the child's head., and painting projects can be put on an easel or taped to a wall. Board games should be placed so that the child has to reach, fully extending the arm during play. When reading or working on projects, items should be placed at eye level to avoid keeping the head bent over for a long period of time.

All children with JRA with joint swelling and pain should avoid the following activities:

1. Contact sports (football, basketball, hockey, soccer)

2. Prolonged running if joints in the legs are involved (soccer, track)

3. Activities that cause repeated stress to the involved joints (legs—jumping rope, basketball, jumping from heights, hopscotch, trampoline; arms and hands—handstands, headstands, cartwheels, volleyball)

4. Prolonged sitting or standing (longer than 20 to 30 minutes)

5. Prolonged static positioning of the hands if they are involved

With the right activities, the child with arthritis can be free to be involved in physical activity and recreation with her peers.

Physical Education and Recess Guidelines

I. Recommended Indoor Activities

Ping Pong

Pool/Billiards

Video Games

Cards

Board Games

Baking

Macrame

Moderate Dance Activities

Needlepoint

Crewel Embroidery

Models/Construction Sets

Fly Tying

Kite Making

Ceramics

Stamp/Coin Collecting

II. Recommended Outdoor Activities

Tricycle/Bicycle

Large Push/Pull Toys

Pedal Toys

Throwing and Catching
(beach ball, Nerf, Frisbee)

Swimming/Water play

Hide and Seek

Shooting Baskets (H.O.R.S.E.)

Tennis, Golf (check with doctor)

Relay Races

Kite Flying

Badminton

Whiffle Ball

Hiking/Nature Walks
(short distance)

III. Activities to Be Avoided

A. Contact competitive sports

Football

Boxing

Karate

B. Activities that cause a "jarring effect" that should be avoided when joints are swollen and painful

Jump Rope

Trampoline

Headstands

Handstands

Cartwheels

Jumping from heights

Aerobic Dancing

Basketball

Volleyball

Hopscotch

Running

Soccer

Appendix E

Summer Camps
for Children with Arthritis

This list includes camps that have been held in recent years. Check with the camp or your local chapter of the Arthritis Foundation for current information.

ARKANSAS

MED-CAMPS AT CAMP ALDERSGATE, Little Rock, AR
This one-week camp is for children ages 7 to 16. Cost is $250 per camper and camperships are available. For details contact Rosemary Eoff, Arthritis Foundation's Arkansas Chapter, 6213 Lee Avenue, Little Rock, AR 72205, (501) 664–7242.

CALIFORNIA

CAMP ESPERANZA, Fawn Skin, CA
Two five-day sessions are offered. Cost is $10 per child and camperships are available. This camp is accredited by the American Camping Association. For details contact Fran Goldfarb, Arthritis Foundation, Southern California Chapter, 4311 Wilshire Boulevard, Los Angeles, CA 90010, (213) 938–6111.

CALIFORNIA

CAMP STEPPING STONE, Julian, CA
One six-day session is offered for children ages 8 to 18. Cost is $50 per child and camperships are offered to lower cost to $10. The camp is in the San Diego foothills. For details contact Dave White, San Diego Area Chapter, 7675 Dagget, Suite 330, San Diego, CA 92111, 1-800-422-8885.

COLORADO

JUVENILE ARTHRITIS SUMMER CAMP, Estes Park, CO
This five-day camp is for children ages 7 to 18. Cost is $175 per child and camperships are available. For details contact Peggy Dibban, National Jewish Hospital & Research Center, Rocky Mountain Juvenile Arthritis Center, Dept. of Pediatrics, 3800 Colfax Avenue, Denver, CO 80206, (303) 398-1378.

INDIANA

CAMP DEL-JA-RI, Indianapolis, IN
This one-week camp is for children ages 8 to 14. Cost is $125 per child and camperships are available. For details contact Julie Marsh, Director, Jameson Camp, Inc., 1100 W. 42nd Street, Indianapolis, IN 46208, (317) 923-3925.

IOWA

CAMP SUNNYSIDE, Des Moines, IA
Three one-week sessions are available for children ages 5 to 18, ages 5 to 14, and ages 13 to 20. Cost is $300. For details contact Nancy Waddell, Program Coordinator, Arthritis Foundation, Iowa Chapter, 8410 Hickman, Suite A, Des Moines, IA 50322, (515) 278-0636.

KANSAS

KANSAS CEREBRAL PALSY RANCH, Eldorado, KS
Several one-week camps are available throughout the spring and summer for children and adults ages five and up. Cost is $250 per camper and camperships are available. For details contact Kelli Poulos, Arthritis Foundation, Kansas Chapter, 1602 East Waterman, Wichita, KS 67211, (800) 362-1108 (Kansas residents only: (316) 263-0116).

MISSOURI

JOINT ADVENTURE, CHILDREN'S MERCY HOSPITAL,
Kansas City, MO
Contact person, Katherine Madson, M.D.

MONTANA

CAMP LIMBERLIMBS, Bozeman, MT
This one-week camp is for children ages 7 to 18. Cost is $100 per in-state child and $125 per out-of-state child. Camperships are available. For details call Trish Rodriquez at (406) 587-4501.

NEW HAMPSHIRE

CAMP DARTMOUTH-HITCHCOCK, Fairlee, VT
This one-week camp is for children ages 8 to 15. Cost is $250 (subject to change) and camperships are available. For details contact Linda Smith, Administrative Assistant, Section of Connective Tissue Disease, Dartmouth-Hitchcock Medical Center, Maynard Street, Hanover, NH 03756, (603) 646-7700.

NEW YORK

CAMP OAKHURST, Oakhurst, NJ
This camp offers two three-week sessions for children ages 8 to 18 and two three-week sessions for adults ages 19 and up. Cost is determined on a sliding scale ($1,200 down) and camperships are available. For details contact Martha Jaffe, New York Service for the Handicapped, 853 Broadway, Suite 605, New York, NY 10003, (212) 533-4020.

OHIO

CAMP WEKANDU, Cincinnati, OH
This one-week camp is for children ages 7 to 21. Cost is $249 per child and camperships are available. For details contact Edith Shear, Special Treatment Center, Children's Hospital Medical Center, Elland and Bethesda Avenues, Cincinnati, OH 45229, (513) 559-4676.

OKLAHOMA

CAMP STRETCH-U-MORE, Guthrie, OK
This one-week camp is for children ages 7 to 16. Cost is $50 per child and camperships are available. For details contact Michele Pitt, Development Director, Arthritis Foundation, Oklahoma Chapter, 2915 Classen Boulevard, #325, Oklahoma City, OK 73106-5450, (405) 521-0066.

PENNSYLVANIA

CAMP HOLIDAY TRAILS, Charlottesville, VA
This camp offers three two-week sessions for children ages 7 to 17. Cost is determined on a sliding scale ($900 down) and camperships are available. For details contact Karen Caggiano, Director of Patient Services, Arthritis Foundation, Western Pennsylvania Chapter, 428 Forbes Avenue, 2401 Lawyers Building, Pittsburgh, PA 15219, (412) 566-1645.

TEXAS

TEXAS CAMPERS, San Antonio, TX
This camp offers three two-week sessions and a one-week session for children ages 7 to 16. No fee. For details contact Jeff Benjamin, Regional Pediatric Rheumatology Center, Texas Children's Hospital, P.O. Box 20269, Houston, TX 77225-2931, (713) 798-2931.

WISCONSIN

CAMP M.A.S.H., Wisconsin Dells
This four-day camp is for children ages 9 to 15. Cost is $125 and camperships are available. For details contact Nancy Tarantino, Program Consultant, Arthritis Foundation, Wisconsin Chapter, 8556 W. National Avenue, West Allis, WI 53227, (414) 321-3933.

Appendix F
=

Summer's Nearly Here: "Think Camp!"

Several Arthritis Foundation chapters and other organizations offer summer camps specifically designed for children and teens with arthritis. Some even offer scholarships to campers from their chapter area. For more information, contact the organizations listed

STATE	CAMP	DATES	CONTACT
Alabama (Dadeville)	M.A.S.H.	8/25-27	Shannon Short* 205/979-5700
Arizona (Amado)	Cruz V	6/19-25	Becky Rebenstorf* 602/290-9090
Arkansas (Little Rock)	Aldersgate	8/6-11	Karen Schneider* 501/6647242
California (Big Bear)	Esperanza	Sess I: 8/12-16 Sess II: 8/16-20	Jennie Abbott* 213/954-5750
California (Julian)	Stepping Stone	7/9-14	Jennifer Warner*
Colorado (Estes Park)	Juvenile Arthritis Camp	7/22-27	Joan Hollister 303/777-2791

*Denotes Arthritis Foundation chapter staffperson.

STATE	CAMP	DATES	CONTACT
Florida (Miami)	Funrise	8/6-12	Gayle Brody* 305/563-0027
Hawaii (Oahu)	JRA Camp	8/17-20	Cookie O'Brien 808/945-7725
Massachusetts (Fairlee)	Dartmouth-Hitchcock	8/20-26	Dartmouth-Hitchcock 603/650-7700
Michigan (Various locations)	Michigan Camps for People	July-August	Pam Assistance Center** 517/371-5897
Ohio (Lebanon)	Wekandu	8/13-18	Pam Heydt 513/559-4676
Vermont/ N New York (Fairlee)	Dartmouth-Hitchcock	8/20-26	Ann Christiano 603/650-7700
Virginia (Charlottsville)	Holiday Trails	7/23-8-4	Karen Caggiono-McMahon* 412/566-1645
Wisconsin (Wisconsin Dells)	M.A.S.H.	8/12-16	Cindy Jackson* 414/321-3933
Wyoming (Estes Park)	JA Summer Camp	6/18-23	Joan Hollister 303/777-2791

*Denotes Arthritis Foundation chapter staffperson.

**Michigan lists 71 camps available for people with special needs.

Appendix G

Arthritis Foundation Chapters

Alabama Chapter

Dixie Kuykendall
200 Vestavia Pkwy, Ste. 3050
Birmingham, AL 35216
205/979-5700; 800/783-7896
Fax: 205/979-4172

Alaska Unit

c/o Sandy Lyons
National Office
Ext. 6264

Central Arizona Chapter*

Carol Chamberlain
711 E. Missouri Ave., Ste 119
Phoenix, AZ 85715
602/264-7679;
Fax: 602/264-0563

Southern Arizona Chapter*

Richard M. Brown, Ed.D.
6464 E. Grant Rd.
Tucson, AZ 85715
602/290-9090; 800/444-5426
Fax: 602/290-0652

Arkansas Chapter*

Diane Stephenson
6213 Lee Avenue
Little Rock, AR 72205
501/664-7242; 800/482-8858
Fax: 501/664-6588

Northeastern California Chapter*

Joan A. Stevie, Exec. Director
3040 Explorer Dr., Ste. 1
Sacramento, CA 95827-2729
916/368-5599; 800/571-3456
Fax: 916/368-5596

*Chapters that provide at least one AJAO activity

  All names listed are chapter presidents unless otherwise noted.

Northern California Chapter*

Judith McAbee
203 Willow St., Ste. 201
San Francisco, CA 94109
415/673-6882; 800/464-6240
Fax: 415/673-4101

San Diego Chapter*

Dolores Gieseke
9089 Clairemont Mesa Blvd.
 Ste. 300
San Diego, CA 92123
619/492-1090; 800/422-8885
Fax: 619/4929248

Southern California Chapter

Bob King
4311 Wilshire Blvd., Ste. 530
Los Angeles, CA 90010
213/954-5750
Fax: 213/954-5790

Colorado/Rocky Mtn. Chapter*

Theodore Zerwin
2280 So. Albion St.
Denver, CO. 80222-40906
303/756-8622; 800/457-6447
Fax: 303/759-4349

Connecticut Chapter*

Ronald Nelson
35 Cole Spring Rd., Bldg. 400
Rocky Hill, CT 06067
203/563-1177; 800/541-8350
Fax: 203/563-6018

Delaware Chapter

Laurie McArthur
222 Philadelphia Pike, Ste. 1
Wilmington, DE 19809
302/764-8254; 800/292-9599
Fax: 302/764-1820

Metro Washington Chapter

Joseph Odda
4455 Connecticut Ave., NE
 Ste. 300
Washington, DC 20008
202/537-6800
Fax: 202/537-6859

Florida Chapter*

John P. Grooms
5211 Manatee Ave. West
Bradenton, FL 34209
813/795-3010
Fax: 813/798-3659

Georgia Chapter

Phil Bonner, Pres/CEO
Pharr Road
Atlanta, GA 30305
404/237-8771; 800/933-7023
Fax: 404/237-8153

Hawaii Chapter

Carol Appelbaum
Penthouse, Honfed Bank Bldg.
45-1144 Kamehameha Highway
Kaneohe, HI 96744
808/235-0120

Idaho Chapter

c/o Sandy Lyons
National Office
Ext. 6264

Central Illinois Chapter

Gary M. Dutro
2621 N. Knoxville
Peoria, IIL 61604
309/682-6600
Fax: 309/682-6600

Greater Chicago Chapter*

Tom Fite
111 Wacker Dr., Ste. 1928
Chicago, IL 60601
312/616-3470
Fax: 312/626-9281

Indiana Chapter*

Marva Cobb
8646 Guion Rd.
Indianapolis. IN 46268-3011
317/879-0321; 800/783-2342
Fax: 515/278-2603

Iowa Chapter*

Thomas Richart
2600 72nd, Ste. D
DesMoines, IA 50322
515/278/0636; 800/622-5015
Fax: 515/278-2603

Kansas Chapter*

Doris Newman
1602 East Waterman
Wichita, KS 67211
316/263-0116; 800/362-1108
Fax: 316/263-3260

Kentucky Chapter

Karen Smith-Lanigan
410 W. Chesnut St., Ste 750
Louisville, KY 402022325
502/585-1866; 800/633-5335
Fax: 502585-1657

Louisiana Chapter

Don Bell
10473 Olad Hammond Hwy.
Baton Rouge LA 70816-8417
504/929-9551; 800/923-2974
Fax: 504/387-6986

Maine Chapter

Woody Woodward
930 Brighton Ave.
Portland, Me 04102
201/773-0595; 800/639-6650
Fax: 207/761-9735

Maryland Chapter*

Vaneeda Bennett
1777 Reisterstown Rd., Ste. 175
Baltimore, MD 21208
410/602-0160
Fax: 410/602-0420

Massachusetts Chapter*

Joanne Donaghue
29 Crafts St.
Newton, MA 02158-5829
617/244-1800; 800/776-9449
Fax: 617/965-3855—588-7686

Michigan Chapter

Paul J Baxendale
23999 Northwestern Hwy.
  Ste. 210
Southfield, MI 48075-6820
810/350-3030; 800/968-3030
Fax: 313/948-8196

Minnesota Chapter

Gary Berg
1730 Clifton Place, Ste., A1
Minneapolis, MN 55403
612/874-1201; 800/333-1380
Fax: 612/874-9332

Mississippi Chapter

Sally Walton
6055 Ridgewood Rd.
Jackson, MS 39211
601/362-6283; 800/844-8400
Fax: 601/874-9332

Eastern Missouri Chapter

Charlie B. Silva, Jr.
8390 Delmar Blvd.
St. Louis, MO 63124-2100
314/991-9333
Fax: 314/991-4020

**Western Missouri/
Greater Kansas Chapter**

Annette Baswell
100 Pennsylvania Ave. Ste. 400
Kansas City, MO 64105-1336
816/842-0335
Fax: 816/842-0335

Montana Chapter

c/o Sandy Lyons
National Office
Ext. 6264

Nebraska Chapter*

Ellen Wright
7101 Newport Ave. Ste. 304
Omaha, NE 68152
402/572-3040
Fax:402/572-3048

Nevada Chapter

Lezlie Barnson
3850 W. Desert Inn Rd., #108
Las Vegas, NV 89102
702/367-1626: 800/395-3724
Fax: 702/367-6381

New Hampshire Chapter*

Alexis Walker
21/2 Beacon St., #10
Concord, NH 03301
603/224-9322; 800479-0077
Fax: 603/224-3778

New Jersey Chapter

Lucy Doree
200 Middlesex Turnpike
Iselin, NJ 08830
908/283-4300
Fax: 908/283-4633

New Mexico Chapter

Nicole Smith/Pres. & CEO
P.O. Box 8022
124 Alvarado S.E.
Albuquerque, NM 87108
505/265-1545; 800999-8022
Fax: 505/265-1547

Central New York Chapter

Linda Brunk-Coddington
5858 East Molloy Rd. #123
Syracuse, NY 13211
315/455-8553

Genessee Valley Chapter

Barbara Kiley
2423 Monroe Ave.
Rochester, NY 14618
716/271-2010
Fax: 716/271-2764

Long Island Chapter*

Patrick T. McAsey
501 Walt Whitman Rd.
Melville, NY 11747
516/427-8722
Fax: 516-427-3546

New York Chapter

Rosario P. Alfieri
67 Irving Place
New York, NY 10003
212/477-8310
Fax: 212/529-9342

Northeastern New York Chapter

Ronald K. Loy
1717 Central Ave., #105
Albany, NY 12205
518/456-1203
Fax: 518/869-3123

Western New York Chapter

Peter A. Filocamo
2440 Sheridan Dr., #201
Tonawanda, NY 14150
716/837-8606

Carolinas Chapter

Debbie Mikysa
Building 7, Ste. 217
Woodlawn Green Office Park
Charlotte, NC 28217
704/529-5166; 800/883-8806
Fax: 704/529-0626

Dakota Chapter (North)

Julie Nesseth
115 Roberts St.
Fargo, ND 58102
701/237-3310
Fax: 701/237-4034

Central Ohio Chapter

Lee Hess
1460 W. Lane Ave.
Columbus, OH 43221
614/488-0777
Fax: 614/488-6418

Northeastern Ohio Chapter

Geraldine Fein
108 Ambassador Dr.
Akron, OH 44132-4407
216/798-5725: 686-9276
Fax: 216/798-5728

Southwestern Ohio Chapter

Sidney Wittenberg
7811 Laurel Ave.
Cincinnati, OH 45243
513//271-4545
Fax: 513/271-4703

Eastern Oklahoma Chapter*

Hope Sutherland
4520 So. Harvard, #100
Tulsa, OK 74135
918/743-4526; 800/400-4526

Oklahoma Chapter*

Suzi Hunter
2915 N. Classen Blvd., Ste. 325
Oklahoma City, OK 73106-5450
405/521-0666

Oregon Chapter

Erin Knight-Haig
4412 S.W. Barbur Blvd., Ste. 220
Portland, OR 97201
503/222-7246; 800/283-3004
Fax: 503/2225542

Central Pennsylvania Chapter

Ronald E. Fritz
P.O. Box 668
17 So. 19th St.
Camp Hill, PA 17011
717/763-0900
Fax: 717/763-0903

Eastern Pennsylvania Chapter

Peter Corrado
Architects Bldg., Ste. 1905-15
117 So. 17th St.
Philadelphia, PA 19103
215/665-9200; 800/322-9040
Fax: 215/665-9249

Western Pennsylvania Chapter

Jerry Ellis
Warner Center, 5th floor
332 Fifth Ave.
Pittsburgh, PA 15222
412/566-1645; 800/522-9900
Fax: 412/391-1677

Rhode Island Chapter

Lori DiPersio
37 No. Blossom St.
East Providence, RI 07914
401/434-5792
Fax: 401/434-5779

Tennessee Chapter

Charles Taylor
Midtown Plaza
1719 West End Ave., Ste. 303-W
Nashville, TN 37203
615/320-7626
Fax: 615/320-7399

North Texas Chapter*

Paula C. Hughes
2824 Swiss Ave.
Dallas, TX 75204
214/826-4361; 800/442-6653
Fax: 214/824-5842

Northwest Texas Chapter

Marty Cook
3145 McCart Ave.
Fort Worth, TX 76110
817/926-9928; 800/283-7733
Fax: 817/926-7735

South Central Texas Chapter

Cindy Walker
4118 McCullough, #18
San Antonio, TX 78212
210/829-7573; 800/284-2438
Fax: 210/829-4246

Texas Gulf Coast Chapter

Tom McCarrick
7660 Woodway, Ste. 540
Houston, TX 77063-1528
713/785-2360; 800/364-8000
Fax: 713/785-6805

Utah Chapter

Lisa B. Fall
1733 South 1100 East
Salt Lake City, UT 84105
801/486-4993; 800/444-4993
Fax: 801/466-1022

**Vermont &
Northern New York Chapter**

Bruce Erwin
P.O. Box 422
2 Church St., Ste. 3F
Burlington, VT 05402
802/864-4988

Virginia Chapter

Kathleen Barrett
3805 Cut Shaw Ave., Ste 200
Richmond, VA 23230
804/359-1700
Fax: 804/359-4900

Washington State Chapter

Carl Jones
100 So. King, #330
Seattle, WA 98104-2864
206/622-1378
Fax: 206/622-1378

West Virginia Chapter

c/o Sandy Lyons
National Office
Ext. 6264

Wisconsin Chapter

Judy Haugsland
8556 W. National Ave.
West Allis, WI 53227
414/321-3933
Fax: 414/321-0365

Index

Rheumatoid arthritis, 1, 12, 63
   adult diagnosed, 63, 117
   See also Juvenile rheumatoid arthritis
Rheumatoid Factor (RF), Positive, 17
Rheumatoid personality, Discussion, 16

School, 1, 56–57, 99–112
   attitude towards handicapped,
      56–57, 75–77, 100–104, 108
   checklist for special needs students,
      106–110, 112
   communication with personnel,
      106–112
   exercise program, 75–77
   fiscal problems, 104
   importance of, 99–101
   Individual Education Plan (IEP), 57,
      101, 112
   legal rights for handicapped, 46,
      101–104, 112
   long range plan, 104, 105
   physical education, 56, 102, 111
   relationships, 99, 111
School liaison program, 56–57, 106
   See also Teachers
Schwarzenegger, Arnold, 72
Schlagel, Roni, 73
Self–esteem, 4, 25, 113–115, 131
Services, xv, 8, 51
   accessing, xv, 51, 60, 103
   community–based, 56–61
   See also: School
Sleep disruption, 66, 67–68, 69
Social worker, 49, 50–51, 102
Special education counselor, 49, 53
Spiritual strength, 9, 32–33
Splints & braces. See Juvenile Rheuma-

   toid Arthritis, Motion
Stress factor, 8, 12
Support groups, 30, 41, 61
Surgery, 26, 33
Systemic JRA, 14, 18–21

Teachers, 25, 56–57, 75, 102, 106–112,
      189
   expectations of JRA students, 25,
      56–57
   relationships with students, 111
Team, Specialized Health Care, 5, 22,
      43, 46–55, 57, 59–60, 119
   educational function, 46, 56, 106
   family partnership in, 48–49, 57, 81,
      126
   how to find, 43, 46
   recreational events, 60
   role with school, 57, 106
   See also: Coordinated care, Nurse,
      Nutritionist, Occupational Ther-
      apist, Physicians, Physical Ther-
      apist
Transportation, Special, 58
Treatment. See Medications; Muscle
      preservation; Physical Therapy;
      Team, Specialized Health Care;
      Splints & braces

Vacations, Family, 39–41

Water beds, Benefits, 23, 67, 71
Weather, Influence on JRA, 22
White, Dr. Pacey, 118
Withers, Angela, 25

Ziebell, Dr. Beth, 108

About the Authors

KATHY ANGEL

Kathy Cochran Angel is a parent of a child with JRA and has served as President of the American Juvenile Arthritis Organization (AJAO), organized and chaired the first annual conference for this group, and served on various committees for the Arthritis Foundation, including Government Affairs and Public Relations. She has been on the Board of Directors of the Texas Gulf Coast Chapter of the Arthritis Foundation and is currently a director of the Southern California Chapter. She has testified before a congressional committee requesting an increase in funding for the National Institute for Arthritis and Musculoskeletal Diseases, and has spoken before many groups on behalf of children with rheumatic diseases. When the AJAO decided to create three awards for excellence, one was named after her to honor a parent who has contributed at the national level to improving the lives of children with arthritis.

EARL BREWER

For over 30 years he devoted his professional life to caring for children with arthritis. He helped develop the concept of team care that is so essential. Other innovative achievements include development of methods to study medicines for children with arthritis as founder and chairman of the Pediatric Rheumatology Collaborative Study Group. He was the leader for 16 years of the successful National Institutes of Health USA–USSR scientific cooperation program for rheumatic diseases in children. Four major studies were completed and published by pediatric rheumatologists in both countries working together. He also was a founder and first chairman of the Rheumatology Section of the American Academy of Pediatrics and a founder and former chairman of the pediatric rheumatology council of the American College of Rheumatology. Dr. Brewer was the founder and director of the Rheumatology Center at Texas Children's Hospital and the Rheumatology Section, Department of Pediatrics at Baylor College of Medicine for more than 30 years. He also was founder and chairman of the Department of Pediatrics at the Kelsey-Seybold Clinic for more than 25 years. Awards include the Surgeon General's Exemplary Service Award in 1988 and creation of an award in his name by the AJAO and the Arthritis Foundation to annually honor a pediatric rheumatologist for innovative contributions.

Earl and his wife, Ria, live in Houston in an old farmhouse in the middle of the city. All of their children are out of the nest. Earl recently retired from the practice of medicine and writes nonfiction and fiction full-time.